SOUL MATCH

SOUL MATCH

PREPARE YOUR BRAIN WITH HYPNOSIS TO FIND
SOMEONE WHO'S REALLY RIGHT FOR YOU

BY

KURT GASSNER

My-mindguide.com

Soul Match
Kurt Gassner

Impressum
My-mindguide – The publishing trademarke of trendguide
Capital GmbH, Klenzestr. 42a, 80469 Munich, Germany.

Reg. Nr. HRB Munich 206639, VAT 152 123 159, CEO:
Kurt Friedrich Gassner
Web: www.my-mindguide.com, mail: gassner@my-mindguide.com

Paperback ISBN: 978-3-949978-00-5
Ebook ISBN: 978-3-949978-01-2
Hardback ISBN: 978-3-949978-02-9

Table of Contents

Chapter 7

Hypnosis And The Mind

Chapter 8

Some Life Story about Hypnosis Love

A Note From The Author

As you dive into the pages of this book, you'll realize that the focus is on hypnotherapy. Why? Well, let's break it down. The unconscious mind holds all our inner treasures, responsible for 95% of our mindset. This means that our unconscious mind is incredsibly powerful in all that it can offer us, dictating the way we perceive life, the way we perceive others, and, most importantly, the way we perceive ourselves. However, the challenge is often learning to unlock the treasures that our unconscious mind contains. Too many of us often feel like we're following a treasure map that leads us nowhere. But with the right tools and the right approach, our unconscious mind can become accessible, making the possibilities we face limitless.

And so, when we consider this concept alongside the idea of finding a soulmate, we begin to see an interconnection. To find a soulmate, attract the right people, and be confident in who we are and what we bring to the table, we can employ hypnotherapy strategies that can lead us to a sense of inner freedom and happiness, attracting those with positive mindsets, goals that align with ours, and mindsets that are just as powerful as our own. This is what I did, and through this process, I uncovered that I am capable of much more than I ever expected—all I had to do was unlock that part of my mind. And so, since the unconscious mind holds 95% of our mindset, we cannot ignore the importance of tapping into this source to find true love, our soulmate, and our life partner. These pages will teach you how to do just that.

Prologue

Upon meeting your soulmate, every part of your mind and body will recognize that this is the right person for you. My goal is to share my personal story to demonstrate the wonder and blessing that I hope you will one day encounter. I hope one day, you can also share how you met and discovered your soulmate.

My story began when I met my wife, whom I have been married to for 37 years now. I met her at a Kitzbüheler Alpen ski cabin. She mocked me the very first interaction we had, as she had initially mistaken me for someone else. I was waiting on a chairlift when I observed her with a friend and invited her and her companion to meet me at the next hut. After they agreed, I skied down effortlessly. The two ladies came minutes later, and I had a lovely talk with both of them. Since I needed to return to Munich later that day, I arranged for a taxi to pick me up shortly after our conversation. But before I left, I asked her for her phone number and scribbled it down while I sat in the backseat of the cab.

"You'll remember 2211," she smiled.

On Wednesday of that same week, I found myself swamped with work at my advertising agency, so I called her in hopes of relieving some of the stress I was experiencing. I curiously invited her to a business meeting with essential clients scheduled for Friday at 7 p.m. She agreed. On Friday, I met with my clients, who were all men, followed by the arrival of Annelise, who was beautiful, sporty, and sophisticated. Everybody's eyes were glued to her. We talked as though we had known each other our whole lives, similar to the kind of first dates you'd see in the movies.

As we sat down for supper, we found our feet gravitating toward one another beneath the table. We left immediately following finishing our dinner and having impressed the client, too. Annelise walked into my car without saying a word, and we immediately began kissing one another with a passion that seemed to be couped up inside us our whole lives. We then made our way to her vast estate, where we spent the night together. I discovered the following morning that she was married to an English gentleman and lived in the United Kingdom.

There have been numerous obstacles and hurdles in our way, but we've overcome every single one; we've been together ever since, and we have two beautiful children, a grandchild, and 37 years of memories in our beautiful marriage. Despite all, we remained united. She abandoned a life of luxury, including a beautiful mansion, and embarked on a new path of hard work just to be with me.

FEAR MODEL

PrimTrigger/Adventures
Anger.
Anxiety.
Sadness
Negative Beliefs
I'm unlovable
Feeling overwhelmed, vulnerable, abandoned/out of control
Pain
I'm inadequate.
Basic Fears
I'm weak.
To be Alone
Primal Fears
Not Enough
I'm a failure
Memories tied to a traumatic event.
I'm pathetic.
Loss of Control
I am not enough.
Loneliness. Muscle tension
My-mindguide.com

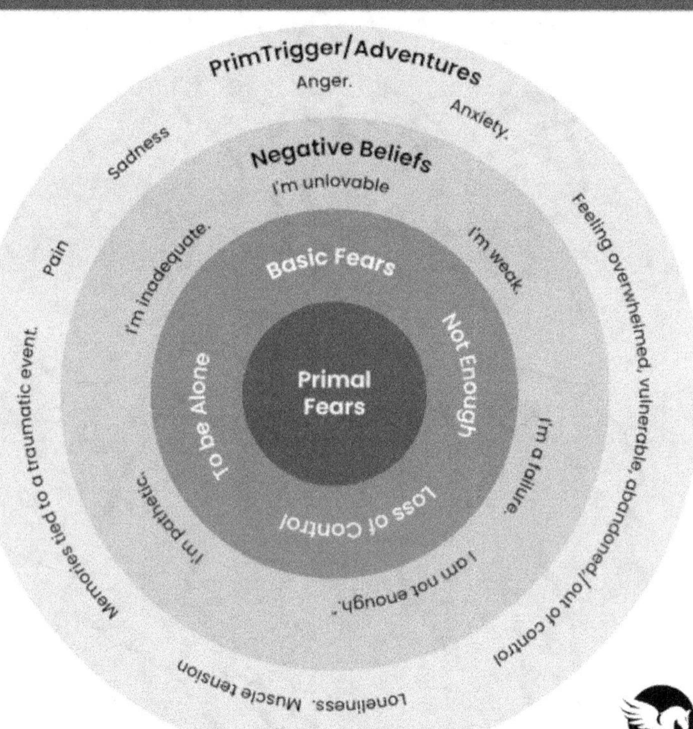

Chapter 1

How Does The Soul Match?

W hat do we understand about the arcane term *soulmate*? First, let us consider what a soulmate *is not*.

A soulmate is not someone with whom you share everything. While you must agree on critical principles and attitudes on life, the misconception that your personality and hobbies must be a perfect fit is untrue. Indeed, sometimes contrasting personalities foster the best partnerships, as they counterbalance one another. However, this is not always the case, and should not make or break the deal when you meet someone you feel could be your life partner.

A kindred spirit is not someone with whom you always agree or disagree. On average, soulmates have as many disagreements as any other human relationship; the difference lies in how they resolve these disagreements and prevent them from devolving into something unpleasant. This is much easier to do in a soulmate connection, as soulmates can understand each other's emotional and psychological concerns more clearly, realizing that their disagreements are insignificant compared to the love and care they have for one another. If the disagreement is significant, then soulmates will find a way to compromise, landing on a solution that works for them both.

Soulmates are not attached at the hip. While they spend more time together than the usual couple, they cherish their independence and recognize that each person is unique. Otherwise, this relationship becomes unhealthy and ventures into toxic territory. In a good soulmate relationship, both partners view themselves as valuable additions to the lives of the other, rather than as a necessary element.

SO, WHAT IS A SOULMATE THEN?

A kindred spirit is someone with whom you feel you could spend every day, and you wouldn't have it any other way. It is someone who understands and values your authentic self, not the exterior persona you present daily. Even during a disagreement, a kindred spirit can readily see past this appearance and feel your true self. A kindred spirit is someone with whom you feel entirely at ease and wish to share everything (sadness and joy, feelings, income, your history, plans, etc.). Your soul partner experiences what you feel; they cannot be happy unless you are and vice versa.

Note that this definition of a soulmate heavily relies on the way a person *feels*. It is, in fact, a critical component of the description of a soulmate. A kindred spirit empathizes with you. You are inextricably linked at the fundamental level of the subatomic particles that comprise you both.

Chapter 2

The Soulmate Connection

As with any issue, there is a wealth of material circulating concerning soulmates, and many of them are contradictory. It's tough to have a firm grasp on what these deep ties signify in our life.

The fairy tale interpretation is that someone out there was created specifically for you, and once you finally find that person, your life will be complete. You anticipate that when you meet your soulmate, everything will be perfect; you will fall madly in love and wholeheartedly support one another in your pursuit of a better life. This is the type of love narrative for which films are made. That is why romantic comedies are so popular. That is why we are drawn to fairy tales.

Another belief system teaches us that we have numerous soulmates who are not all romantic or sexual in character. A soulmate might be a close friend, a family member, or a romantic partner. There are also many kindred souls in life with whom we will cross paths.

For this investigation, we focus on the romantic chemistry that leads us to assume we've discovered a kindred soul. When we meet this individual, we believe that our prayers have been answered, that our dreams have come true, and that we have finally completed our match. No one else we've met has had such an effect on us. We have never felt so in love—so insane for someone—in our lives.

The issue with finding this type of soulmate is that when we're crazy in love with someone, the emphasis is more on the crazy part rather than the love part. The focus is not on the calm, centered, balanced, self-assured, confident, and controlled feelings we experience; in fact, we often experience the exact opposite when we fall so madly in love with someone. We become unstable, confused, unsure of ourselves, and battling low self-esteem. We can't help but wonder why we feel so insignificant compared to the brilliance this person exudes.

We remain steadfast alongside this person in hopes of overcoming obstacles and discovering the pot of gold at the end of the rainbow: the promise of true love and married bliss. However, the longer we continue down this path, the more our self-esteem erodes, and the deeper we appear to sink into darkness.

Is this love? Is this the soulmate connection? What is it?
While some are fortunate to find someone with whom they have a genuine, positive tie of love and their relationships are peaceful and inspiring, others discover that their soulmate relationships are the most problematic and challenging relationships they've ever encountered. They experience a

great deal of pain and sorrow. The promise of a fulfilled dream becomes the most significant nightmare. Mr. Right morphs into Mr. Wrong. The prince transforms into a frog. Snow White becomes the evil stepmother.

How are we duped into believing that the person we fell in love with is our soulmate? And why do we have such a difficult time letting go of this person when we realize we may have had it all wrong?

I believe that there is a possibility of a soulmate connection there. We share a profound soul connection with this person, even though the relationship has grown unpleasant, and we feel highly uncomfortable, if not abused. This is due to something we call *karmic resolution*.

The soulmate hypothesis is predicated on the belief that in a previous life, we were together with that person, which is what made us recognize our connection in this life. It may appear as though we know the person and experience an instant spark. *"How did we become acquainted with this individual previously?"* is the question. Were they our husband, wife, or lover? Were they someone we cherished? Or is it possible that this person was someone we wronged in the past and is now wronging us to even the karmic scales? This person likely mistreated you previously, and you drew them back into your life to hurt you again so that you could learn to say "no" to abuse.

Is this person someone with whom a bond of true love may have existed in previous lives, but this lifetime has left them with so many deep wounds that they cannot open their hearts and allow love to enter? And no matter how hard you try to love and help them, you end up being the one who suffers because they are incapable of genuinely loving you in return?

Did you sign a soul contract with someone that required you to meet them to learn some critical life lessons? Your task may be to develop a greater love for yourself in the face of someone who appears incapable of loving you. Alternatively, it could be learning the ability to honor and respect yourself in front of someone who does not praise you. There may be a significant part of your soul development at work here.

And so, keeping these possibilities in mind, we begin to understand that finding a soulmate does not always imply that you have found the love of your life—the one you were born to be with and who was born to be with you. It could be excruciatingly painful to undergo such experiences, but it may also be necessary to learn the valuable lessons that these painful experiences bring. These are lessons you may not choose to learn and may encounter significant resistance to. On the other hand, your soulmate may be even more resistant to the lessons you've come to impart. They may do everything possible to escape seeing the reality in front of them. They could be incapable of committing to the road of love because they were taught that love hurts, thus protecting their heart with defensive walls. No matter how much love you give, you will never be able to penetrate their walls.

Soulmates might join us for a moment, a cause, or for the rest of our lives. However, we can be confident of one thing: When we encounter a kindred spirit, we are never the same again. They arouse something within us that we are incapable of sleeping through, even if we wanted to. We can go forward, abandon them, or be abandoned by them, but they will always be a part of us. In its aftermath, we may be forced to learn lessons of forgiveness, letting go, and self-love in ways we never imagined. Perhaps we need to realize that sometimes loving someone requires letting go. But even if we learn to let go, we will never forget them or their impact on our lives.

The lover with whom we lack tremendous chemical attraction may be the most peaceful relationship of all, but we must transcend our yearning for intense chemical interest. Intense romantic or sexual chemistry might imply volatile emotional relationships. It can seem intoxicating and thrilling at first, but it eventually gives way to something that destabilizes us. There is a cause behind the intensity.

Therefore, rather than seeking someone who will disrupt your world, it may be prudent to seek someone who will soothe your emotional oceans and give you peace. This is a much more significant component of an enduring love for someone you can rely on in the long run.

Chapter 3

There Are 5 Ways To Tell If You've Found Your Soulmate

It's tough to discern whether you've found your ideal match and whether the person you're seeing is truly your soulmate, especially when you're still in the beginning stages of a relationship. However, specific signals indicate whether the person you're dating is your perfect match.

1) **You are comfortable and relaxed with this person, as if you've known them for a long time:**
   Soulmates frequently have the impression that they already knew one another before the meeting. Esoteric studies of soulmates claim that soulmates met previously, in another life. Whether or not you buy into this claim doesn't quite matter; what matters most is that soulmates share a fundamental energy from the start. They have no explanation for it, yet it appears as though they have known one other longer than they have. They have a sense of security around one another as if they could say or do anything without

judgement. The level of comfort among kindred spirits is exceptionally high.

2) You're in it for the long run

Soul partners do not wait three days after a first date before contacting the other. Even early in the relationship, soulmates do not play hard to get, nor do they pretend to care less about their spouse than they genuinely do. Soulmates are not scared to appear desperate in front of one another when they make a move, and they are not at all reserved about their feelings for one another (whether they verbalize it or not). Soulmates' primary aim is to be with one another, and they are unconcerned with what other people think, much less how they should behave at any given point in the relationship. They simply do what feels right.

3) You feel a deep connection with this person right from the start:

As previously mentioned, soulmates share a fundamental energy bond that is often apparent early on in the relationship. This can be defined as the sensation that this individual is virtually a part of you (not to be confused with passion, where you feel you need the person to keep living, so to speak). You feel as though this person contributes to the quality of your life, and you want to share significant events with them.

4) Your most important life values match:

Generally, soul partners agree on all critical life decisions. This implies that they share a range of values—spiritual and worldly—and decide on various issues together based on those values, such as where they should live, how they should spend their money, or what their overall goals should be, both personal and professional. They do not have to share the same interests, but they should share the most important ones, at least. What this means that each marriage is unique.

5) **When you make love, you are deeply sensual as well as extremely passionate and satisfied:**
Physical manifestations of love between soulmates are just as strong as their emotional and spiritual connections. When soulmates meet physically, it is more than a sexual act. It is the manifestation of profound spiritual connection. This is why the intensity and amount of passion between soulmates are significantly higher than the level of affection between typical couples. The profound connection you sense will undoubtedly be expressed externally in a soulmate relationship.

HOW TO ATTRACT YOUR SOULMATE

Prepare your brain with hypnosis to find someone who's right for you

FIND A SOULMATE

Do you dream of finding a soulmate, someone who will complete your life?

Do you wonder if this person exists, and whether there's any hope of finding him?

Many people are convinced that there is an ideal person out there, someone who is destined to be their genuine life partner, their soulmate. And many are similarly persuaded that when you meet that person (as fate will have it), you will magically know who it is; it will be blindingly, irrefutably evident that you have now discovered the one destined for you.

GET READY FOR LOVE

Perhaps you want to find the love of your life, marry, and begin a family. Or maybe you choose the security and companionship of a committed relationship.

You may, however, maintain self-defeating and pessimistic views about love and your capacity to discover it. By now, you've probably recognized that your thoughts and beliefs in this area are impeding your progress.

You may have convinced yourself that you're incapable of maintaining a healthy relationship, and that all the good people out there have already been claimed. But what's problematic here is that these beliefs foster a pessimistic mindset that can drive love away and undermine an otherwise good relationship before it even begins.

HYPNOSIS CAN HELP

I've worked with numerous individuals over the years who were willing to abandon their self-limiting ideas and believe that love was possible for them.

Hypnosis is a powerful technique that can assist you in increasing your self-esteem, enjoying the present moment, being focused on the direction of a relationship, and trusting in your capacity to love.

Some have transformed themselves from abusive relationships to fantastic, caring, and rewarding ones. This is the power of your mind at work when your energies are focused.

Best of all, even if love does not find you immediately, you will have a richer, happier, and more satisfying life when you are not fighting for someone you haven't even met yet.

ABOUT HYPNOSIS:

Hypnosis Defined: Hypnosis is a natural but altered consciousness marked by concentrated attention and increased sensitivity to suggestion. It is a state that results in a condition of regulated imagination.

Being hypnotized is like being engaged in a beautiful book or film, or experiencing the sensation of being in the midst of an excellent massage. You are comfortable, but you are aware of your surroundings. You are not dozing off or out of it.

It is easy to make significant and lasting changes while in this state, as the subconscious mind readily adopts new beliefs. More than any other technique, hypnosis demonstrates the strength of our thoughts and opinions.

Even when all other options have failed, hypnosis can help.
After over two decades of witnessing the power of our minds firsthand, I feel that hypnosis should be the first—not the last—tool in everyone's toolbox.

Why bother with patches, gum, and steam when hypnosis can assist you in quitting smoking in as little as two or three sessions?

Why spend months or even years attempting to overcome flying or public speaking phobias when hypnosis may significantly diminish—if not wholly eradicate—such worries in as few as three to six sessions?

Why strain and become disappointed with weight loss when hypnosis can help you eliminate sweets and carbohydrates in only one or two sessions, changing your entire connection to food?

Even if you've been battling for years and have exhausted all other options, hypnosis can help you achieve your goals in a relatively short period.

Once your thoughts change, your life will change, too.
Hypnosis exemplifies the strength of belief. For us, what we think to be true is true. If we can re-direct the subconscious mind, it will faithfully obey.

Therefore, if we can persuade the subconscious mind that it no longer desires candy or cigarettes, its behavior will change accordingly.

Numerous studies have established that the subconscious mind cannot distinguish between a vividly imagined experience and an actual event. This enables you to envision and rehearse novel behaviors and emotions. Hypnosis is a highly effective tool for altering fundamental ideas, attitudes, and modes of thought. And as our beliefs change, our attitudes, responses and emotions change, as well.

FREQUENTLY ASKED QUESTIONS ABOUT HYPNOSIS

WHAT IS HYPNOSIS?

Hypnosis is defined as an altered state of consciousness marked by heightened sensitivity to suggestion and focused imagination. Although relaxation is frequently associated with hypnosis, it is not required.

HOW DOES HYPNOSIS WORK?

While in hypnosis, all irrelevant information is tabled, and our attention focuses exclusively on a single goal or image. This level of thought and emotion allows us to pour all our energy towards change, dispelling limiting beliefs, and drawing tremendous forces to our aid.

Consider the difference between the sun's diffused energy and the sun's concentrated energy in a laser beam to get a sense of how hypnosis works. Your conscious mind is analogous to the sun, while your hypnotic ideas are analogous to the laser beam.

ARE THERE ANY SIDE EFFECTS?

There are only favorable side effects in hypnosis, such as improved sleep and an overall sense of wellbeing. Indeed, the primary benefit of the work I undertake is improved sleep. Clients frequently say that their road rage has subsided, their coworkers are no longer getting on their nerves, and they feel more content. Thousands of case studies demonstrate that hypnosis is a safe, natural, and effective change method.

CAN I BE HYPNOTIZED?

YES, YES, YES. Most people are hypnotizable. Indeed, we are all in and out of hypnosis throughout the day. If you've ever driven past your exit on the highway, daydreamed during a meeting, or become absorbed in a good book, you've experienced a moderate form of hypnosis. Moderate hypnosis is sufficient for most of the work we undertake, including weight loss, smoking cessation, and overcoming fears of public speaking. We do not require depth to reach success.

With nearly two decades of experience, I've only had a few customers who did not enter a trance on the first session. Success, on the other hand, was gained in future sessions.

Therefore, if you have been informed that you cannot be hypnotized, be skeptical. Perhaps your hypnotherapist did not employ successful inductions, or you do not have a rapport with that particular physician. Or maybe you need to be a little more patient with yourself and practice.

ARE SOME PEOPLE MORE HYPNOTIZABLE THAN OTHERS?

Yes. Hypnosis is a skill like any other, and some are naturally gifted at it. The good news is that everyone improves with practice. That is why it is critical to train in self-hypnosis on your own. I have seen numerous individuals who have been told that they could not be hypnotized to attain trance.

CAN HYPNOSIS HELP ME?

While hypnosis is neither a panacea nor a substitute for medical or psychiatric treatment, it has been demonstrated to be beneficial for various ailments, from exam anxiety and bad habits to procrastinating and improving test scores. Therefore, the chances are good that it will benefit you, as well, whether you choose to utilize hypnosis exclusively or in conjunction with other therapies prescribed by your doctor or therapist.

WHAT IS THE DIFFERENCE BETWEEN HYPNOSIS AND MEDITATION?

Hypnosis is referred to as goal-directed mediation. Meditation soothes the mind and is helpful in and of itself. However, there are no constructive objectives, perspectives, or images during meditation. We first calm the mind and relax the body with hypnosis, then incorporate mental imagery, positive ideas, and other treatments, such as NLP or part therapy. There is always a purpose in hypnosis.

WHAT SHOULD I LOOK FOR IN A PROFESSIONAL HYPNOTIST?

Consider hiring a hypnotherapist who has completed training at a state-licensed school and is a member of at least one professional hypnotist organization. Currently, Illinois does not have any legislation requiring training. In other words, anyone can hang a title and call themselves a hypnotist. Therefore, inquire about qualifications. Even if someone has a certification, consider that certification requirements differ significantly.

Unfortunately, many consultant hypnotists have recently completed a weekend training course or, worse, a self-study program. These professionals are frequently ill-equipped to provide excellent service to their consumers. Bear in mind that verifying a doctor's credentials is in your best interest.

Along with training, other considerations are the hypnotherapist's years of experience, expertise with your condition, and rapport.

IS HYPNOSIS REAL?

Hypnosis is a legitimate form of psychological therapy. It is commonly underused and misinterpreted. Medical study is ongoing to investigate how and when hypnosis can be used as therapy.

WHAT EXACTLY IS HYPNOSIS?

Hypnosis is a form of treatment that can assist you in coping with and treating a variety of conditions.

To accomplish this, you will be guided into a deep level of relaxation by a professional hypnotist or hypnotherapist (sometimes described as a trance state). They can give suggestions to help you become more receptive to therapeutic changes or improvements while you are in this state.

Trance states are common. If you've ever found yourself out of breath while watching a movie or daydreaming, you've experienced a similar trance condition.

Actual hypnosis or hypnotherapy is not performed on stage as entertainment.

IS HYPNOSIS THE SAME THING AS HYPNOTHERAPY?

Yes and no. Hypnosis is a form of therapy that can treat a wide range of conditions. Hypnotherapy is the application of this technique.

How does hypnosis work?

A trained hypnotist or hypnotherapist induces hypnosis by producing a state of extreme focus or concentrated attention. This is a guided approach that uses verbal signals and repetition.

While the trance state into which you enter may appear comparable to sleep in many respects, you remain completely aware of what is occurring.

While you are in this meditative state, your therapist will provide guided recommendations to aid you in achieving your therapeutic goals.

When the session is complete, the therapist will either awaken you, or guide you to exit the trance state on your own.

It is unknown how this level of intense inner concentration and focused attention has such a strong effect, but research in this regard is ongoing.

Hypnotherapy may plant the seeds of new concepts in your mind while you are in a trance state, and these changes quickly take root and flourish.

Additionally, hypnotherapy can prepare the path for more in-depth processing and acceptance. If you are confused in your natural state of mind, your mind may be unable to accept suggestions and directions.

WHAT HAPPENS TO THE BRAIN DURING HYPNOSIS?

Fifty-seven people's brains were investigated under guided hypnosis by Harvard researchers. They found that during hypnosis, two parts of the brain responsible for processing and directing what happens in your body are most active.

Similarly, under hypnosis, the portion of the brain responsible for your actions and the area responsible for your awareness of those acts appear to be detached.

Different regions of the brain are visibly influenced during hypnosis. The areas that contribute to activity management and public awareness are the most impacted.

Is it all just a placebo effect?

Hypnosis significantly alters brain function. This indicates that hypnosis affects the brain in a distinct way from the placebo effect.

As with hypnosis, the placebo effect is based on suggestion. Guided talks or any behavioral therapy can significantly impact behavior and feelings. Hypnosis is one of these therapeutic techniques.

ARE THERE ANY SIDE EFFECTS OR RISKS?

Hypnosis is rarely associated with any side effects or hazards. If administered by a trained hypnotist or hypnotherapist, and it may be a safe alternative therapeutic option.

Some persons may suffer the following mild to moderate adverse effects: headache somnolence dizziness situational anxiety

On the other hand, hypnosis for memory recall is a contested practice. Anxiety, discomfort, and other adverse effects are more prevalent in individuals who employ hypnosis in this manner. Additionally, you may be more prone to fabricate memories.

Do doctors recommend the practice?
Certain physicians are skeptical that hypnosis can cure mental illness or physical discomfort. While the evidence supporting the use of hypnosis continues to grow, not all physicians agree with its benefits.

Numerous medical colleges do not train physicians in hypnosis, and not all mental health professionals receive training throughout their academic years, either. As a result, healthcare experts have many misconceptions regarding this putative therapy.

WHAT CAN HYPNOSIS BE USED FOR?
Hypnosis is frequently promoted as a cure-all for various ailments and problems. The research supports the use of

hypnosis for some, but not all, of the conditions for which it is employed.

Research demonstrates compelling evidence for the use of hypnosis to treat:
Aches
Irritable Bowel Syndrome
Post-Traumatic Stress Disorder
Insomnia

There is insufficient evidence to claim that hypnotherapy can help treat the following conditions:
Depression
Anxiety
Smoking
Post-surgical wound healing
Weight loss

Additional research is necessary to determine the efficacy of hypnosis in treating these disorders, amongst others.

But most importantly, and as this book focuses on, hypnosis can be used to attract your soulmate. Since hypnosis is such a powerful tool in transforming our mind and our thoughts, we can harness its energies to attract the type of people we want in our lives—the people we want as our life partner. And so, to do this, a hypnotist will walk you through your dream partner, helping you determine the qualities you want in a man or woman, and grounding your dreams in reality. Through this experience, you will have a chance to dig deep within yourself, improve your self-esteem and confidence, and go out in the world in search of love—ready for a healthy relationship to flourish.

WHAT HAPPENS DURING A HYPNOTHERAPY SESSION?

You cannot be hypnotized during your initial consultation with a hypnotist or hypnotherapist. Instead, the session is dedicated to discussing your objectives and the approaches that the hypnotist may take to assist you.

Your therapist will aid you in relaxing in a comfortable setting during a hypnosis session. They will walk you through the process and evaluate your session objectives. They will then guide you into the trance state using repetitive verbal prompts.

While you are in a responsive trance state, your therapist will prescribe that you work toward specific goals, support you in visualizing your future, and coach you in making healthier choices. Following that, your therapist will awaken you from your trance.

IS ONE SESSION ENOUGH?

While one session may be practical for specific individuals, most therapists recommend beginning with four to five sessions. Following this step, you might discuss the number of additional sessions required. Additionally, you can discuss the necessity of maintenance sessions.

FACT VS. FICTION: DESTROYING 6 POPULAR MYTHS

While hypnosis is gradually gaining acceptance in traditional medical practices, some fallacies continue. Here, we distinguish between fact and fiction.

MYTH: EVERYONE CAN BE HYPNOTIZED

Not everyone is as susceptible to hypnosis as others. Around 10% of the population, according to one study, is exceptionally hypnotizable. While the remainder of the population is sensitive to hypnosis, they are less likely to adopt the approach. However, as with any skill, with practice, the majority of people can reach a state in which they can achieve hypnosis.

MYTH: HYPNOSIS AND SLEEP ARE THE SAME THINGS

While you may appear to be sleeping during hypnosis, you are awake. You're simply in a state of deep relaxation. Your muscles will relax, your respiration will slow, and you may experience sleepiness.

MYTH: PEOPLE ARE NOT IN CONTROL OF THEIR BODIES WHEN THEY ARE HYPNOTIZED

Hypnosis does not entail a sleep state, in which individuals are not aware of their actions. Although it involves extreme relaxation, individuals are still fully in control of their bodies and movements and are aware of their surroundings.

MYTH: PEOPLE CAN'T LIE WHEN THEY'RE HYPNOTIZED

Hypnotism is not a panacea for truth. You are more receptive to suggestions under hypnosis, but you retain your free will and moral judgment. Nobody can compel you to say anything you do not want to say, whether the statement is true or false.

MYTH: YOU CAN BE HYPNOTIZED ONLINE

Numerous smartphone apps and Internet videos encourage self-hypnosis, but they are mainly ineffective.

Researchers in a 2013 study discovered that these products are not designed by a qualified hypnotist or hypnosis group. As a result, physicians and hypnotists warn against their use.

PROBABLY A MYTH: HYPNOSIS CAN HELP YOU "DISCOVER" LOST MEMORIES

While it is possible to recall memories under hypnosis, you are more likely to generate false memories while in a trance state. As a result, many hypnotists remain suspicious of hypnosis' ability to aid memory recovery.

The End Result

Hypnosis perpetuates stage performance tropes, complete with cackling chickens and daring dancers.

However, hypnosis is a legitimate therapeutic therapy that can be used to treat variousmedical issues. This encompasses sleep disorders, depression, and pain management.

You must work with a certified hypnotist or hypnotherapist to have confidence in the guided hypnosis procedure. They will develop a strategy to aid you in accomplishing your unique goals.

10 REASONS TO GET HYPNOTIZED

Why Should You Be Hypnotized?

YOU ARE TRYING TO QUIT SMOKING (AGAIN)

To quit smoking is one of the most common reasons individuals seek hypnotherapy. They've usually tried nicotine patches and gum before deciding to try hypnotherapy, both of which were unsuccessful. Indeed, the National Center for Complementary and Integrative Health cites studies that support the use of hypnotherapy (in conjunction with other treatments) to help smokers quit.

YOU CAN'T GET A GOOD NIGHT'S SLEEP

Insomnia and other sleep disorders affect millions of individuals worldwide. Hypnosis help individuals identify the source of sleeplessness and suggests techniques to relax and soothe your thoughts, allowing you to sleep. Hypnotherapy is also frequently used to treat children's sleep disorders, such as nightmares, sleepwalking, and night terrors.

YOU ARE TRYING TO OVERCOME A PHOBIA OR FEAR

Fears and phobias affect people of many ages and may even interfere with daily living. For instance, frequent concerns that people try to overcome include spiders, heights, elevators, snakes, flying, and needles. Hypnotherapy can help someone who is preparing for an international flight or even looking to donate blood.

YOU ARE SEARCHING FOR LOVE

Hypnotherapy can be used as a tool to visualize and attract your soulmate, addressing your subconscious beliefs that may be attracting you to the wrong men, leaving you heartbroken every time.

YOUR ANXIETY OR STRESS IS OUT OF CONTROL

Everybody is subject to stress and anxiety. However, it can seize control of the body and mind of certain people, stopping them from living the life they want to live. Hypnotherapy for anxiety can help you identify underlying issues and provide solutions for improved stress management.

YOU WANT TO RETRIEVE MEMORIES FROM THE PAST

Our minds do not recall all our events in great detail, especially if they include a catastrophic occurrence in our lives that we want to suppress. Hypnotherapy can be highly effective at eliciting the disclosure of previously suppressed memories, allowing individuals to confront and overcome them.

YOU ARE TRYING TO LOSE WEIGHT

Weight loss is an individual experience. And while some people may have legitimate health concerns, a large portion of weight loss success is determined by the mind, not the body. Hypnosis can address this, making life adjustments and temptations more manageable.

YOU HAVE A BIG JOB INTERVIEW COMING UP

Communication and public speaking may be a significant source of worry for many people, even more so when under duress. Many people use hypnosis to practice and improve their communication skills in preparation for an important job interview.

YOU WANT TO STOP BITING YOUR NAILS

Nail-biting is one of the most prevalent bad habits that people try to break but cannot on their own. This is because most nail biters begin as children, and the problem persists throughout adulthood. Hypnotherapy can help in addressing the physical consequences of nail-biting to help you quit.

YOU HAVE CHRONIC, DEBILITATING MIGRAINES

It's normal to get a headache every now and then, but those who suffer from chronic migraines frequently struggle to get out of bed. Studies have found hypnosis to effectively treat migraines without the adverse side effects associated with drugs.

THE IMPORTANCE OF HYPNOTHERAPY

Hypnotherapy is not about an elderly physician flashing a clock in your face and whispering, "Listen to my voice." It is another non-pharmacological way of analysis and therapy recommendation for individuals who experience common difficulties that can be managed without medications.

Although hypnotherapy has been used to improve awareness since ancient times, it is a genuinely groundbreaking tool for treating various mental disorders and persistent behaviors. Hypnotherapy is merely an altered state of consciousness in which you appear to be sleeping or in a trance but are entirely aware of your surroundings and what is happening around you at the time. You can hear and record everything a hypnotherapist says to you; the ideas that alter your behavior or thought process. In most situations, individuals who practice hypnosis in Melbourne offer a variety of hypnotherapy treatments for smoking cessation, weight loss, anxiety reduction, and resolving other issues.

FOR SELF-IMPROVEMENT:

An increasing number of people are experiencing issues with low self-esteem and insecurity. It is difficult for these individuals to obtain a solid job and maintain a relationship, causing them to become frequently become disoriented in social situations. Hypnotherapy clinics in Melbourne provide therapies that aim to resolve this issue by highlighting and using a person's positive characteristics rather than focusing exclusively on the negative characteristics and traits contributing to depression.

FOR SELF DETERMINATION:

Nothing is more discouraging than failing to pursue your dreams and ending up not doing something you believe you should be. Fears, prior failures, individuals, and particular events influence how we view ambition and goal attainment. That is why many hypnotherapy practitioners in Melbourne place a premium on dismantling people's negative thought processes to pave the way for more direct goal fulfillment.

FOR OVERCOMING BAD HABITS:

Hypnotherapy is rapidly gaining popularity as a means of resolving harmful behavioral habits. One of the most common reasons people in Melbourne seek hypnosis is to quit smoking. Other possible reasons include resolving unhealthy behaviors such as overeating, excessive spending, or sleep problems.

FOR ADDRESSING BELIEFS STOPPING YOU FROM FINDING LOVE

Returning to our discussion on soulmates, hypnotherapy can be used to break down subconscious beliefs you've harnessed inside you that may be contributing to a pattern of unhealthy relationships. For those with emotional trauma that has largely gone unaddressed, it may be crucial to dig deep within to determine which subconscious thoughts are leading you away from love, and replacing these thoughts through hypnotherapy with ones that will finally lead you toward love.

TOP 10 BENEFITS OF HYPNOTHERAPY

Hypnotherapy is a sort of therapy that uses the power of suggestion to help individuals make positive changes in their lives. For many, it is a highly efficient kind of treatment with several benefits, ranging from stress relief and relaxation to quitting harmful behaviors like smoking and gambling.

Depending on your reasons for pursuing hypnotherapy, it may take just one session or several sessions to see beneficial change. Additionally, you will discover self-hypnosis skills that will enable you to continue your treatment long after the sessions have ended.

The top ten benefits of hypnotherapy:

1. **IT CAN HELP YOU QUIT SMOKING:**
    Even if you smoke 100 cigarettes a day or have smoked for 60 years, hypnosis is one of the most effective methods for safely and painlessly quitting smoking without cravings.

2. **IT CAN HELP YOU CHANGE YOUR EATING HABITS:**
   If you want to lose weight without dieting, this is an excellent approach. Hypnotherapy accomplishes this by removing impediments to success, such as emotional eating, negative thoughts and sentiments about your body, and cravings for unhealthy snacks. Increasing your passion for nutritious food, drink, and exercise can be a long-term solution and helpful method to maintain a healthy lifestyle.

3. **IT CAN HELP YOU STOP DRINKING:**
   If you cannot stop drinking alcohol via willpower alone, hypnotherapy is a highly effective method of abstinence. Hypnosis is one of the most powerful methods for swiftly, securely, and naturally breaking bad habits, undesired behaviors, and addictions.

4. **CAN RELIEVE STRESS:**
   Stress reduction using hypnosis is one of the simplest methods for achieving deep relaxation. It is a highly effective method of enhancing your health and well-being, leaving you calmer, more optimistic, and completely rejuvenated.

5. **IT CAN HELP YOU ACHIEVE SUCCESS:**
   Reprogram your mind to achieve success in all aspects of your life, whether financial, romantic, creative, or motivational, boost your confidence and self-esteem, or envision and experience a better future. Nothing is impossible.

6. **IT CAN HELP YOU OVERCOME FEARS AND PHOBIAS:**
   Fears and phobias can obstruct and constrain us in our daily lives. Our unconscious minds' fundamental duty is to

protect us from emotional suffering and bodily injury, which develops these issues. We may resolve, release, and rewrite the past by taking you back to the event, cause, or experience that generated this issue.

7. **IT CAN ALLEVIATE THE SYMPTOMS OF IBS:**
Fears and phobias can obstruct and constrain us in our daily lives. Our unconscious minds' fundamental duty is to protect us from emotional suffering and bodily injury, which develops these issues. You may resolve, release, and rewrite the past by returning to and recalling the event, cause, or experience that generated this issue.

8. **CAN HELP WITH ANXIETY AND DEPRESSION:**
Our harsh self-criticisms may generate or exacerbate anxiety and despair. Each day, we have approximately 50,000 thoughts, many of which are harmful. Hypnotherapy is a highly effective method for reshaping the negative thinking patterns that keep us locked in places we don't want to be and moving us toward more positive, empowering, life-affirming ideas and behaviors.

9. **CAN HELP WITH NATURAL HEALING:**
Each thought you have has a tangible consequence in your body, affecting all 50 trillion of your cells. Use your mind's power to heal your body. When the Marisa Peer method of quick transformation therapy is used to command and instruct our cells to return to their ideal objective, specific unexpected effects can occur.

10. **IT CAN HELP YOU FIND YOUR SOULMATE:**
When you work toward improving your self-esteem and confidence, you begin to attract others who are on your

same level, especially considering that we get what we put into the universe. Hypnotherapy can help you in multiple ways to attract you soulmate; primarily, however, it can help you visualize the partner you want to spend our lives with, ensuring you're clear on the characteristics you're after. Then, hypnosis can help you come to grips with the reality of your situation, while also ensuring that you find inner happiness before searching for external happiness. Your soulmate will ultimately be attracted to your mind, thoughts, and positive energy, all of which hypnotherapy can help you harness.

HYPNOSIS SIGNS

A hypnotic subject may encounter a variety of occurrences. The following is a list of common outward indicators in hypnosis. Not everyone experiences these symptoms when in a trance; therefore, one should not rule out hypnosis if some indications are lacking. Numerous hypnotic clues are subtle, and only an experienced hypnotherapist can detect them; the individual in hypnosis or an observer may completely miss them.

- **BODY**

  The subject's muscles relax, and they try to become more comfortable. A hypnotic subject is not physically tense. Relaxation of the muscles is more visible in facial expressions. In hypnosis, a person's face is smooth and toned, often accompanied by a vague hollowness in the eyes.

  Although a person does not have to be frozen to enter a trance, a person in hypnosis does not engage in frantic movements, such as wringing their hands or swinging their feet. Even persons who routinely have tics or spasms do not typically experience them while under hypnosis. When a person is in a trance, they move slowly and efficiently. Body heat is also a sign of hypnosis.

- **EYES**
When someone enters a trance, they begin blinking more slowly.

The eyelids flicker during the early trance period. This is an unmistakable indicator of hypnosis. Sometimes, the eyeballs roll up, revealing only the whites of the eyes. Many individuals experience teary eyes and redness, as well.

Although it is not visible from the outside, a person in a trance frequently describes blurred vision. Additionally, hypnosis might result in tunnel vision or changes in objects' colors, sizes, and forms.

HEADS UP

A person in hypnosis is less likely to be distracted by external sounds. At its most extreme, the individual may become so absorbed inside that he ceases to listen to the hypnotherapist.

PULSE AND BREATHING

Although the pulse rate and breathing rate fall, a person entering hypnosis may experience a transient increase in pulse and breathing rate due to discovering they are in hypnosis.

TO SWALLOW

During trance, the swallowing reflex weakens or disappears entirely. Naturally, if this is brought to the person's attention, the subject will usually gulp.

PSYCHOMOTOR PROCESSING

Often, a period passes between when a suggestion is made and when the individual in hypnosis makes it.

---

13 WAYS TO START TRAINING YOUR SUBCONSCIOUS MIND TO GET WHAT YOU WANT

Here are a few strategies for retraining your mind to be an ally, not an adversary.

1. **BE WILLING TO SEE THE UNCHANGEABLE CHANGE:** The first step in enacting significant change in your life is not believing that it is possible but rather being willing to investigate whether it is.

   You will not be able to transform from a total skeptic to a wholehearted believer overnight. A happy medium between the two opposite ends of the spectrum is simply being receptive to what might be possible. Perhaps send a few "scary emails" in which you propose something to a client or partner that they do not need to reply to. You may have a few dozen unanswered messages, but someone will ultimately respond.

   The point is that you're willing to investigate whether something is conceivable. That's what will alter the course of your life.

2. **PERMIT YOURSELF TO BE SUCCESSFUL:**
   Rather than regurgitating the same story about being happy once you lose ten pounds, get a promotion, and experience two significant life events, concentrate on shifting your inner monologue to something like this: "I enable my life to be good."

   Allow yourself to be happy and prosperous without feeling guilty about it. If you have a subliminal association with success being immoral or corrupt, you are unlikely to take the necessary steps to live your desired life. Rather than that, allow yourself to enter a whole, happy, healthy, grounded, and purposeful existence.

3. **DON'T ALLOW OTHER PEOPLE'S FEARS TO CAST SHADOWS OF DOUBT:**
   The way people react to your accomplishment reveals how they are doing in their lives.

   If you announce your engagement, those already married and happy will rejoice for you. Folks who are dissatisfied with their marriages may tell you that it is difficult and that you should make the most of your remaining time as single individuals.

   The argument is that other people's anxieties are self-referential projections of their circumstances. They have nothing to do with your capability or incapacity.

4. **SURROUND YOURSELF WITH POSITIVE REINFORCEMENT:**
   Refrigerate a bottle of champagne. Change the message on your morning alarm to "CONGRATULATIONS!" Ascertain

that the items you see and touch regularly convey positivity and hopefulness. Keep a post-it note with an inspirational message next to your computer. Unfollow individuals who consistently post negative messages and follow those who post positive statements and exciting pictures. Make your newsfeed a location that can stimulate your growth, rather than one that diminishes your sense of value.

5. **SPEAK YOUR SUCCESS AS A PRESENT FACT, NOT A FUTURE PLAN:**
    Though you should avoid statements such as "I drive a convertible" or "I am a CEO" if they are not true, you should begin discussing what you want out of life, not in the context of one day pursuing it, but as a life you are already living.

    Rather than saying, "I want to do that someday," add, "I am currently strategizing how to do it." Rather than thinking, "I'll be happy when I'm at a different place in my life," consider, "I am capable of being happy right now; no one is holding me back."

6. **CREATE A VISION SPACE:**
    Being able to envision what you want out of life is critical for its creation because if you don't know where you're headed, you won't know which direction to go first.

    Once you have a crystal-clear mental image of what you want and how you want to live, you can begin to enact and create it. If your desires remain vague or conflicted, you won't be able to take meaningful action toward any goals. Create a collection of words and images that symbolize what you desire and how you want to live, whether you use a Pinterest board, blog, journal, or board.

7. **IDENTIFY YOUR RESISTANCE:**
When our subconscious thoughts prevent us from pursuing something we're passionate about, it's because we have a competing belief about it.

To find what you're resisting in your life, question yourself. Consider why you feel better when you procrastinate or why pursuing your true desires may put you in a position of vulnerability. Before proceeding, determine a way to address those needs.

8. **HAVE A MASTER PLAN FOR YOUR LIFE:**
Forget five or even ten-year plans; so much changes over time that setting goals you can keep are practically impossible in that time frame. Most certainly, other or even better possibilities will present themselves, and while your life may not unfold as planned, you will be better off as a result.

Rather than that, create a master plan. Determine your fundamental values and motivations. Consider the ultimate goal of what you wish to accomplish during your lifetime; consider the type of legacy you want to leave. Once you've identified your big picture principles, you may make long-term choices that are consistent with your true self.

9. **START A GRATITUDE JOURNAL:**
The most effective technique to shift your mindset from "wanting" to "having" is to develop a practice of thankfulness

and gratitude. By expressing gratitude for what you have, you may shift your perspective from one of desire for change to contentment with where you are. Nothing attracts abundance more than appreciation. A proverb states that once you believe you have enough, you become receptive to getting more and more. That is unquestionably true.

10. **START ASKING FOR WHAT YOU WANT, EVEN IF YOU KNOW YOU'LL BE DENIED:**
If someone approaches you about taking on a consulting assignment, request the amount of money you genuinely desire for it. If your objective is to advance in your organization, meet with your superior and communicate your ambitions. Contact brands with whom you wish to collaborate. Begin by requesting what you want, even if you have no reason to expect anyone will give it to you. They eventually will. Once you recognize your worth, others will follow suit.

WHERE DID HYPNOSIS COME FROM, WHY USE IT, AND WHAT TO EXPECT

Have you ever tried hypnosis? If not, then let me explain a little about hypnosis and what you may expect, just to put your mind at ease and help you in getting the most out of this compelling approach.

To begin, there are numerous misconceptions regarding hypnosis, and I will discuss some of the most prevalent ones. The most frequently held misconception is that hypnosis is a form of sleep. During the sessions, you will not sleep. Even though the term "hypnosis" is derived from the Greek word

"Hypnos," which means sleep, you will not be sleeping. You may hear everything I say during the session, which is acceptable as long as you remain in hypnosis. In some instances, you may be able to answer, and I may request predefined signs or a verbal response from you. However, I want to emphasize that even if you are conscious of everything you say during the session, rest assured that you are in hypnosis.

It is not an issue if you completely relax and fall asleep throughout the session. You are in a secure location and will not miss any of the session's content. Additionally, there is no need to be concerned about not waking up. This is not possible. Fewer than 10% of the population enter such a profound trance state that they disassociate or blackout as they do during anesthesia. These individuals are called somnambulists, and they do not recall what occurs during hypnosis. Even so, these individuals will awaken after a session.

Your hearing functions similarly to a security camera, which is constantly on guard to ensure the safety of both you and your kids. Consider how quickly a woman wakes up when asleep and hears her baby cry. If someone enters your home while you are asleep, you will awaken immediately upon hearing a disturbance. Your hearing is on 24 hours a day, taking in and recording information. We use this to our advantage in hypnosis so that even if you fall asleep during the session, your brain is still recording all the information in your subconscious mind.

The history of hypnosis is fascinating but lengthy and comprehensive, so allow me to give you the short version to understand where hypnosis comes from and why it is so effective, helpful, and safe for us to use. We'll dive into more details later on.

Hypnosis is at least 6,000 years old; others believe it is far older. Ancient Egyptians, Greeks, Romans, Indians, Chinese, Persians, and Sumerians researched hypnosis and altered states of consciousness. Between the ninth and fourteenth centuries, a thorough grasp of human psychology was developed, and therapeutic techniques such as analysis, altered states of consciousness, and hypnosis were used to alleviate emotional discomfort and suffering.

This occurred before deeming the approach *psychotherapy* and *hypnotherapy* as we know them today. Between the fifteenth and sixteenth centuries, physicians worldwide developed and perfected the concept of hypnosis and its applications.

In the eighteenth century, an Austrian physician named Dr. Frantz Anton Mesmer was the most influential character in creating hypnosis. Mesmer employed magnets and metal frames to execute passes over the patient to remove blockages (i.e., the causes of disease) in the body's magnetic forces, generating a trance-like state. Mesmer quickly achieved similar success by moving his hands over the patient, a technique he coined *animal magnetism*. Regrettably, due to the theatrical nature of his healing sessions, which were conducted in front of the public and medical professionals, his work was mocked, and his tangible results were overlooked. His name, however, remained and entered our lexicon as the verb *mesmerize*.

Mesmer died in 1815, but a student named Armand de Puysegur advanced Mesmer's work. He discovered that the spoken word and direct commands readily allow people to enter a trance so deep that allows physicians to operate without pain or anesthesia.

Dr. James Esdaile of England set the first medically recognized record for surgery performed under a trance when he completed his first operation without anesthetic in India and went on to achieve an incredible 300 significant operations and a thousand minor procedures under hypnosis or mesmerism, as it was still called at the time.

The subsequent development of hypnosis came from a Scottish optometrist named Dr. James Braid. By chance, he realized that by focusing on an object, a person may quickly enter a trance state without the aid of "mesmeric passages." In 1841, he reported his findings and erroneously coined the term *hypnotism* from the Greek word "Hypnos," which translates as "sleep."

The British Medical Association voted in favor of hypnosis in medicine in 1891, but approval did not come until 1955—64 years later! The American Medical Association took notice of a patient who underwent a thyroidectomy, or surgical excision of the thyroid gland, without anesthetic at that time. Hypnosis was the only tool available to alleviate pain. As proved in thyroid surgery, hypnosis is a powerful and valuable tool for blocking pain. Weight management, cigarette addiction, motivation to exercise, improved study habits, nervous habit control, and development of healthy self-esteem are only a few of the conditions that can be positively influenced with therapeutic hypnosis.

Now allow me to address some of your probable worries and answer some questions you may have in response to this information.

Hypnosis can occur only if you want to enter a state of hypnosis. You can be hypnotized only if you consent to it. I cannot approach you and enthrall you without your knowledge or consent. This means that hypnosis is completely safe for anyone who wishes to use it for these purposes and more!

Hypnosis is not a magical mind control technique that deprives you of your will or ability to make rational choices. Hypnosis is a trance-like state of consciousness that makes you more receptive to suggestions and directions aimed at helping you make positive behavioral and physical changes in areas such as weight control, cigarette addiction, motivation to exercise, study habit improvement, nervous habit control, and developing healthy self-esteem. It is one of several types of therapy that can be beneficial in various ways for a wide variety of behavioral and physical disorders.

Hypnosis is not a mind-control technique. You are in control. If I make an incorrect, damaging, or disagreeable suggestion, your mind will reject it, and you will become completely attentive. When under hypnosis, you cannot be coerced into acting against your will or moral code. If something occurs during the session that requires your immediate attention, you will be able to handle it. Simply count to three, and you will be fully awake. Alternatively, you can pull yourself out of hypnosis by simply opening your eyes.

While you may not believe you are in a trance throughout your hypnosis session, you will notice your attention narrowing and your breathing slowing as you begin to relax and approach the alpha state. The alpha is a state of consciousness or trance that is one level below wide-awake or fully conscious consciousness, referred to as the beta state of consciousness. You can become up to two hundred times more receptive to suggestion and direction in the alpha state than you are in full consciousness, or the beta state.

To illustrate the benefits of the alpha state, consider a pipeline connecting the conscious and subconscious minds. Your hypnotist drops the seeds of suggestion into this conduit that you have asked them to plant and assist you with. These recommendations are 200 times more likely to be helpful in the subconscious than what we tell ourselves in our usual beta state. This is because they restructure our cognitive and behavioral bases. They improve our perception. Hypnotic ideas empower individuals to exert greater control over subconscious thinking frameworks that could otherwise permanently impair their lives. Hypnosis is a technique for reorganizing the mind's associations more beneficially and healthily.

Once the therapist has established the ideas and associations, they ensure that nothing else will dissociate them in the future. When a problem is resolved, it is usually resolved permanently. For instance, most weight loss situations can be managed symptomatically. Creating and owning new behaviors would take between one and six sessions or around 21 days. Occasionally, we must go a little deeper to determine the underlying cause of the weight gain when it comes to weight control. This may require multiple sessions. According to an American Health Magazine study, psychoanalysis resulted in a 38% recovery after 600 sessions, behavior therapy resulted in a 72% recovery after 22 sessions, and hypnosis resulted in an astounding 93% recovery after only six sessions. As you can see, hypnosis is both safe and highly effective at helping you rapidly achieve your goals.

Hypnosis is an entirely natural state; it is something you encounter daily. For instance, when you become immersed in a beautiful film or television show, you are in a hypnotic state. If you've ever driven to work or the store and wondered how you got there since your mind was preoccupied with a thousand other thoughts, you've encountered hypnosis. If you've ever been in the zone, a state of complete concentration on the task at hand and nothing else, you've experienced hypnosis. If you've ever found yourself daydreaming, you were most likely in a state of hypnosis. Even when reading an excellent book, you can become so involved in the story that you miss it when someone speaks to you. Your brain then enters a trance-like state known as hypnosis. However, you can also enter a state of hypnosis through soft material that induces a hypnotic mood, such as an uninteresting lecture. It's hard to stay focused when someone speaks in a monotone voice. Perhaps you begin to have more exciting dreams; this is also hypnosis.

Simply keep in mind that you may be aware of everything your hypnotist says during the session, which is normal

because you are still in hypnosis; you can always return yourself to the waking beta state by opening your eyes or counting to three. Most importantly, remember that *you* are always in charge.

WHAT ARE THE DIFFERENT TYPES OF HYPNOSIS

Hypnosis is not a new phenomenon; it has been used for years to astound, impress, and aid in treating and curing many ailments. For years, it was dismissed as a fringe, new-age fad. However, it is now recognized as a natural effect, with mainstream science accepting its applicability. The general public is growing more familiar with it, and the previous cynicism is receding.

The principles of hypnosis are the same regardless of the method used. While some treatments, such as hypnosis, are centuries old, other treatments stem from recent research, and as a result, new approaches have been developed in this regard. Typically, the sort of hypnosis used is determined by the desired objective. Each method has inherent worth and mastering any of them opens the door to the others. The following are the primary categories:

- **TRADITIONAL HYPNOSIS**
  Traditional hypnosis is the most established form of hypnosis and has existed for a lengthy period. It is the version performed by a hypnotist who induces a deep trance in the patient and then guides them through suggestions and directives. This technique is used in stage hypnotism.

  Over the years, the classic hypnosis method has been widely disparaged and criticized—largely unjustifiably—although some criticism is valid. Using stage plants and actors to simulate hypnosis has damaged the conventional hypnosis approach. When used correctly, it is a vital and effective instrument that may be enjoyable and beneficial.

- **HYPNOTHERAPY**

Hypnotherapy is using hypnosis to facilitate healing or positive development in any form. It is frequently used to address psychological issues within the mind. When used effectively, hypnotherapy can reprogram behavioral patterns within reason, controlling phobias, irrational fears, addictions, and negative emotions. Additionally, hypnotherapy may be used to control pain feelings, and hypnosis has been used to perform surgery on fully conscious patients who would be in agony if not for the use of hypnosis.

Hypnosis can be used to assist individuals. Hypnotherapy is used to facilitate positive growth and healing. Hypnosis, when used in hypnotherapy, can also have physical benefits, the most evident of which is blocking pain.

Hypnotherapy is frequently used in conjunction with relatively light hypnosis rather than the deep trance state associated with the classic type. Most patients are completely awake and aware. The critical aspect of hypnotherapy is that the patient must be completely focused on the therapy and attentive to the words spoken by the therapist. Maintaining a positive rapport with the therapist is critical. If the patient lacks faith in the treatment or believes it will fail, the therapy will fail. However, if a patient is optimistic and receptive, the success rate is exceptionally high.

- **SELF HYPNOSIS/AUTOHYPNOSIS**

  As implied by the name, this technique is based on the person inducing hypnosis on themselves. This is accomplished by the subject's acquisition of a set of procedures or through listening to a tape. Most self-hypnosis is administered through hypnotherapy and is comparable to profound relaxation and meditation.

  Self-hypnosis and hypnosis are similar. The critical distinction is that the subject implements their suggestions rather than those of others. The widespread belief is that all hypnosis is self-hypnosis. This is because while the hypnotist may supply the ideas, it is the subject's evaluation and interpretation of these recommendations that determine the outcome. The hypnotist serves as a vehicle for the issue to enter a trance, but the matter is the one who analyzes the information. Regardless of the method, the outcome is the same.

  Self-hypnosis is a technique that can be used. It works in a manner very similar to hypnotherapy and is exceptionally efficient at resolving psychological issues, phobias, stress, and addictions. It is frequently used to induce a state of deep relaxation.

- **NLP HYPNOSIS**

  Some of you may be familiar with NLP or neuro-linguistic programming. This psychological therapy was developed to treat psychological problems, phobias, depression, habits, and learning disorders. While NLP is still frequently employed, it is increasingly used as a self-help technique to support and encourage feelings of wellbeing. This strategy has increased and is now being used by healthcare experts, business professionals, life coaches, and self-help courses.

- **ERICKSONIAN HYPNOSIS**

This hypnosis technique is referred to as secret hypnosis, covert hypnosis, black ops hypnosis, quick hypnosis, and/ or conversational hypnosis. This approach employs normal conversation to induce hypnosis without the subject being aware of it.

Ericksonian hypnosis, or conversational hypnosis, was pioneered by Dr. Milton H. Erickson, a hypnotherapist. Erickson mastered language after contracting polio, which kept him in bed for years. During this time, he honed his technique for inducing hypnotic states without the subject's understanding.

This type of hypnosis can be used on skeptical persons of hypnotherapy or more traditional forms of hypnosis and has been said to be more effective on suspicious individuals.

Incorporating hypnotic language and hypnosis techniques into everyday discourse can rapidly produce a trance. This is a low-level trance state that is quite effective.

This hypnosis technique was initially developed as a hypnotherapy technique but has since gained popularity among everyday people. The strategy enables users to regain control of their lives and employ these tactics in various familiar settings. There are numerous courses available that teach these techniques, suggesting that they can be used to gain control over others. This is somewhat true, and it is apparent that this method of hypnosis is genuine and effective. While the procedure is very straightforward, mastering it will take time.

Chapter 4

Hypnosis Explained (Debunking The Myths)

Hypnosis is a relatively straightforward and easily explained psychological phenomenon - yet it is frequently misrepresented as a form of black magic or false mysticism. Due to this lack of a balanced representation, many dismiss hypnotic wisdom as mere fiction or hogwash; and persons who have been hypnotized are frequently stereotyped as feeble-minded or credulous. However, none of this is true. To summarize, if you're interested in being hypnotized, I hope this clarifies any misconceptions you may have regarding hypnosis.

MYTH 1: HYPNOSIS IS A STATE OF CONSCIOUSNESS
Hypnosis is in no way associated with any particular state of consciousness. The reason individuals mistake hypnosis for a state of consciousness is because we frequently link hypnosis procedures with a half-sleep, half-awake condition. We envision patients lying on velvet sofas, eyes closed, and awareness directed inward toward their subconscious. However, the reality is that hypnosis may be used to expand and constrict awareness.

Stage hypnosis is an excellent illustration of hypnosis acting at "normal" consciousness levels. When a participant clucks like a chicken or acts out a scene from *Saving Private Ryan*, it is not because the individual is unconscious and being pulled along by their strings like a stuffed puppet; instead, they are in a situation where they feel comfortable behaving in a way they would not normally behave in front of a crowd. The hypnotist is not controlling the patient; they are adequately communicating with them. Throughout the session, the participants' free will remains intact. The subject has the option of coming out of hypnosis at any time, but why would they when they are having so much fun pretending?

MYTH 2: ALL HYPNOSIS IS "PLAYING PRETEND."
Participants are fully aware that they are not genuinely a chicken or are not actually in a movie during hypnosis. They are aware of their actions (it just so happens that hypnosis can make people good actors).

However, not all hypnosis can be labeled fake. It is contingent on the nature of the proposals made. If the patient is instructed to "cluck like a chicken," they will do so. If the advice is "remember a period in your past when you felt truly secure," the patient does not imagine it; they are genuinely thinking about it and identifying themselves with that time.

I concur with hypnotists who feel that self-hypnosis is the foundation of all hypnosis. This means that a hypnotist cannot convince someone to act against their will. Compliance is always present on both sides of an encounter. The main distinction is that hypnotists, when they uncover the appropriate channel of communication, can elicit odd or non-ordinary behaviors.

MYTH 3: HIGHWAY HYPNOSIS

Highway hypnosis, as defined by Wikipedia, says,

Highway hypnosis is a state of mind in which a person can drive a truck or automobile long distances, responding appropriately to environmental stimuli with no remembrance of doing so consciously. In this state, the driver's conscious mind appears to be focused entirely elsewhere, processing the massive amounts of information required to drive safely. 'Highway Hypnosis' is merely one expression of a very typical occurrence in which the conscious and subconscious minds appear to focus on different activities; workers performing simple and repetitive jobs and persons who are sleep-deprived are likely to experience comparable symptoms. As so, it functions as a type of subconscious "driving mode."

Again, you may have guessed why this definition is incorrect: hypnosis is not a mental state!

Hypnosis on the highway is a trance condition (it is a shift away from "everyday" awareness). There is no communication taking place, and as a result, there is no hypnosis. Another similar and natural trance state occurs when you become completely immersed in a film and lose track of time.

It's easy to confuse these states with hypnosis, as hypnosis replicates similar trance states to boost suggestibility. (But remember: if no suggestions are being communicated, then it is not hypnosis.)

MYTH 4: HYPNOSIS IS NOT A REAL CATALYST FOR PHYSICAL OR CHEMICAL CHANGES IN THE BODY.

Indeed, just because the brain is composed of electrochemicals called neurons that fire between 50 and 200 times every second, anything can act as a catalyst for a chemical change in the body. All it takes is to think about something to modify our brain chemistry.

However, more practically, individuals want to know if hypnosis may result in physical changes, such as weight gain or loss, muscular growth, or even an increase in breast/penis size. Typically, the answer is "yes, to a degree."

Hypnosis cannot force your body to accomplish something it cannot do naturally. However, hypnosis has been shown to assist the body in undergoing specific changes through the use of suggestion for both behavioral changes (such as eating less or motivating yourself to go to the gym) and even physical changes (changes in metabolism, the time it takes muscles to repair, and there have even been cases of improvements in vision, and yes, penis and breast size growth; hypnosis has been shown to be particularly good with directing substantial changes in soft tissue).

REMEMBER: Hypnosis is beneficial in helping the body reach its full potential; it does not allow you to transcend your biological tendency in some mystical way. However, hypnosis has a high probability of revealing information about your body of which you were previously unaware.

MYTH 7: YOU SHOULDN'T TRY HYPNOSIS WITHOUT A TRAINED HYPNOTIST OR HYPNOTHERAPIST.

Most qualified hypnotists and hypnotherapists will advise you always to consult a specialist. However, it would be disingenuous of me to assert that you must do so when I am entirely self-taught. Indeed, I believe that everyone should learn a little hypnosis to check out and discover the possibilities for oneself.

Hypnosis is a natural occurrence; it is your birthright to investigate it, as well as the mind/ body in its whole. There are many books, podcasts, and videos available to help you start practicing hypnosis; experiment with as many as you like to get a feel for the various techniques and begin discovering the core principles that allow a hypnotist to be flexible and effective.

I would suggest that you begin by experimenting with self-hypnosis techniques. Nothing too sophisticated. Simply practice getting yourself into a state of relaxation or light trance via hypnotic suggestion.

Additionally, you can practice reading generic scripts to a friend or family member and having them read them to you. They are hardly the most valuable items, but they are usually harmless and simple to train with.

Google "free hypnosis scripts" and have a look at some of the straightforward scripts for "confidence" or "relaxation."

Take your studies slowly at first; just gain a feel for the various parts of a hypnosis session: inductions, scripts, and how to exit a session responsibly.

While hypnosis is typically a pleasant experience, things can go wrong. Be comfortable with how to rapidly end sessions if you feel yourself veering off course, especially before diving into some of the more complex tactics, such as adjusting our belief systems or character principles.

HYPNOSIS AND REAL LOVE

When discussing the relationship between hypnosis and love—discussing the ways in which it can be used to attract and find a soulmate—the question often arises of whether the hypnotist is *forcing* the individual to find a soulmate, or whether the individual in search of a soulmate is using hypnosis to force another into falling in love with them. This is very far from the truth, as hypnosis cannot force a person to do something they don't want to do.

What hypnosis can help with is harnessing the mind's energy to attract—naturally—a soulmate. Love cannot be forced, nor can a soulmate relationship. For those wanting to find love naturally, be assured that hypnosis *is* in alignment with finding love naturally. What it offers is knowledge about oneself that goes deeper than the surface. When a person is being hypnotized and engaging with hypnosis, they enter a state of deep relaxation in which their subconscious is at the forefront, letting their thoughts run loose without restriction. This state allows the individual to face thoughts and memories that may be holding them back in life. For instance, an individual may have faced great emotional trauma growing up at the hands of their parents, and thus, their subconscious has come to build a warped idea of what love really is. For this reason, the individual attracts all the wrong partners, thriving off toxicity, drama, and unhealthy patterns, and calling it love at the end of the day. With hypnosis, the individual can recognize and address these thoughts and memories and re-build their core beliefs to align with what they want their future to look like— who they want their life partner to look like.

Using hypnosis to attract a soulmate in no way makes the process unnatural.

Chapter 5

Learn Hypnosis and Its Many Secrets!

That being said, many people today are concerned about the boundaries of hypnosis. There have been so many articles, courses, and other content created on the subject that the borders appear to be perplexing and deceptive. Some learn hypnosis to hypnotize others, while others learn hypnosis to hypnotize friends to exact revenge. There are also individuals who learn hypnosis to better understand their state of mind.

With that in mind, what is hypnosis fundamentally? Hypnosis is a technique in which creating domains of the mind are crossed, wired, and bypassed to reach and create a more rational, analytical, and perceptive environment. Many people want to learn hypnosis for a variety of reasons. I studied hypnosis because I wanted to observe what is true, what is objective and what is subjective in the world of hypnosis. What I gained from the courses I chose was far more than I could have hoped for. For instance, I discovered that one can pre-hypnotize someone; one can even use hypnosis to communicate subliminally, and one can even hypnotize someone while out on a date! Learning hypnosis is not tricky.

There are numerous catalogues, publications, and courseware available online that are all free and offer free hypnosis training; however, some are hoaxes. It's important to be wary of where you get your information.

Returning to the subject at hand, hypnosis is frequently referred to as an altered state of mind or consciousness; however, this is not the case. The majority of alleged hypnotic state indicators suggest that hypnosis can be achieved without the subject relaxing; this is referred to as waking hypnosis and is a potent tool to use while out on dates, attending interviews, closing business deals, or attempting to convince your wife to forgive you, increase your pain threshold, or even reduce pain! For this and countless other reasons, hypnosis continues to be a highly contentious subject, even though anyone interested in learning hypnosis can do so by enrolling in one of the many hypnosis training courses available on the market today. Learning hypnosis is not a waste of time or resources; many people take hypnosis courses as a pastime or learn hypnosis solely to brag.

There are now two theories governing modern hypnosis research: state and non-state hypnosis. State theories emphasize that hypnosis involves an altered state of consciousness and that this altered state is central to hypnosis. Non-state ideas, on the other hand, assert that hypnosis is a complex psychological process, frequently described as the mind's focused attention heightened by anticipation. I realize these are lofty words, but there is a study being conducted in the field of hypnosis, and part of this research results in the development of hypnosis training courses that teach you how to use hypnosis effectively.

What do those who have been hypnotized have to say about the experience? Indeed, roughly 79% of these individuals feel or experience an altered or transformed state of mind; frequently, upon awakening from hypnosis, these individuals report feeling relaxed and calm. Personally, when I was hypnotized—and everyone was required to hypnotize themselves during the first series of practical exercises in the hypnosis training course—I had gone blank as if a switch had been flipped off, and I was mindlessly answering questions. It was more of a sedated state of mind. When I awoke, I felt compelled to act; I was brimming with vitality. I suppose it's energizing to learn hypnosis and experiment with it on yourself. The question now is whether you wish to learn hypnosis.

SOME TRUE FACTS ABOUT HYPNOSIS

Hypnosis is an extreme yet intriguing term that may mean various things to a wide variety of people.

Some individuals visualize the zombie-like trances depicted in Hollywood films, while others may have witnessed hypnosis used in popular areas, such as weight loss and smoking cessation.

However, many of you reading this may be surprised to learn that hypnosis has been accredited by the American Medical

Association for hospital usage since the late 1950s! This is not some bizarre, out-of-date therapy, as its strength and popularity continue to grow. And it appears as though new findings and results from recent studies demonstrating the usefulness of hypnosis are published every week.

I've collaborated with the Hypnosis Live Shop to develop this information for you and to help you debunk some of the most prevalent hypnosis fallacies.

I'm sure you'll find it highly enlightening and indeed quite interesting! So, shall we begin?

"Hypnotists have special powers!"
No, I'm afraid not! While they can produce some impressive outcomes, they are not as cloak and dagger or magical as all those old Hollywood films would have us believe!

Hypnotists do not possess any particular abilities. They have the knowledge and experience to assist you in entering an intense level of relaxation and then communicating the appropriate message to your inner mind, which transforms an idea into action!

All hypnosis is, in effect, self-hypnosis. You are the one who is changing your mental habits. The hypnotist (or the hypnosis recording) only assists you in the process.

"Hypnosis is an occult! And it's against my religion!"
Hypnosis is not esoteric and does not offend any religion. Hypnosis is an entirely safe and natural approach to calming

your mind and inducing positive affirmations and thoughts in yourself.

Hypnosis is a branch of psychology that bears no resemblance to any religion.

"Hypnosis isn't effective at changing anything!"
Thousands upon thousands of satisfied hypnotherapy patients attest to this. Numerous studies have established the efficacy of hypnosis in a wide variety of contexts.

Hypnosis was approved for medical usage by the American Medical Association in 1958, and practically all modern institutions now use it to some extent. It has a documented success rate of 90.6% for quitting smoking when used correctly (School of Medicine at the University of Washington). It was discovered to be more than 30 times more effective than conventional weight loss methods (Consulting and Clinical Psychology Journal). It was found that it provided immediate' and significant relief to 75% of women who used it to help with IBS symptoms, with an additional 80% reporting improvement six years later (according to the American Psychological Association).

Additionally, it has been shown to alleviate migraines, speed recovery from surgery, decrease pain, aid in the recovery process from drug addiction, alleviate chemotherapy symptoms, and control blood pressure. It is as successful as Ritalin in treating children with attention deficit disorder.

Additionally, thousands of people worldwide have used hypnosis to boost confidence and self-esteem, overcome addictions, overcome previously devastating fears and phobias, finally drop that weight, quit smoking, and increase brainpower, to name a few.

REAL SELF-HYPNOSIS EXPLAINED BY A HYPNOTHERAPIST AND HOW IT DIFFERS FROM SELF-HYPNOSIS

True self-hypnosis occurs when you initiate the hypnotic state and use it to accomplish your aims. True self-hypnosis occurs when you act as your therapist; it happens when you are deeply in a trance and use it to accomplish whatever you like. It is far different from passively listening to a self-hypnosis CD and allowing another person's voice to guide you.

Self-hypnosis that is genuine and active might be compared to surfing a wave; you grab the lock and ride it, steering your board. You harness the wave's energy and ride it to the top. You must first master the art of catching a wave before progressing to mastering the art of riding it. Similarly, you can learn to reach the hypnotic state first and then the strategies for fully using and enjoying the power of your mind.

How can you learn real self-hypnosis?

There are many methods for learning self-hypnosis, multiple schools, and numerous books. Specific approaches, mainly those learned through literature or meditation, can take years to master.

The most effective way to learn self-hypnosis is to do so while in a hypnotic state. In just one session, a trained hypnotherapist can teach you the fundamentals of self-hypnosis. While in a deep hypnotic state, you are offered advice on how to perform the task on your own. Then you complete it under the supervision of the hypnotherapist, who will ensure that you comprehend each step.

Once you've mastered the ability to enter and maintain a hypnotic state on your own, you can progress to more advanced techniques, such as pain control, self-healing, study skills, and awareness-raising techniques. Self-hypnosis is an excellent coaching tool since it enables you to train and practice in the hypnotic state, perfecting the skills.

What are the limitations of self-hypnosis?

Occasionally, a problem may be too complicated to tackle in self mode. If the condition is severe and causes significant personal discomfort, it is preferable to seek expert assistance. When you are profoundly depressed, traumatized, in crisis, or under the influence of a destructive habit, you require outside professional aid that combines counseling and individualized therapy.

Additionally, you must exercise caution when treating the medical issue or alleviating any physical symptoms. It is critical that you do this under medical supervision and inform your doctor whether the symptoms have been eliminated.

How does natural hypnosis differ from listening to self-hypnosis audio?

There are many self-hypnosis CDs available, some of which teach you how to relax. In contrast, others claim to offer assistance and rapid remedies in various areas, including lifetime phobias and past life regression. The hypnosis CDs for relaxation and general wellbeing may be beneficial, and if you enjoy them, continue to do so. However, if listening to them becomes tedious and monotonous, you may want to listen to some pleasant music instead, as you will relax more when you love what you are hearing.

When you listen to a self-hypnosis CD, you simply relax and follow the instructions of another person's voice. Generally, you listen to someone's ideas and, yes, you learn to relax; occasionally, it even helps you cope with the specific issue it promises to assist with. Numerous sophisticated self-hypnosis recordings can lull you into a deep trance—you can have a thrilling ride on the crest of a wave, but this is not self-hypnosis; you are riding in someone else's boat and receiving someone else's solutions.

Listening to a mesmerizing CD can be dangerous at times. You should be aware of the limitations of self-hypnosis before listening to a self-hypnosis CD—particularly more advanced ones that may induce a profound trance. If you are undergoing a traumatic event, severe sadness or anxiety, or have any sort of psychosis, a deep trance may be harmful and can cause significant distress.

The critical distinction between authentic self-hypnosis and listening to a hypnosis CD is the active involvement that authentic self-hypnosis requires. You enter the hypnotic state independently; you employ it in your way, using your particular resources. The experience is quite empowering in and of itself, boosting self-esteem and offering enlightenment.

True self-hypnosis is simple to use and extremely powerful because you are the expert on yourself; you can create the most potent suggestions; you can use your own words that work for you, or you can skip the words entirely and use your imagination. You can feel the recommendations rather than say them.

Self-hypnosis that is genuine and active is the most empowering self-help technique. Each self-help approach is founded on self-hypnosis; each self-help method teaches you how to harness the power of the mind or use suggestions to accomplish goals, and each self-healing method is established on self-hypnosis. When you practice authentic self-hypnosis, you can develop the ability to access all aspects of your mind; you can use your mind to connect with and heal your body; you can access and clear troubling emotions and fears, and you can expand your awareness by accessing the spiritual aspects of your mind.

CAN HYPNOSIS CURE ADHD?

There is a shortage of literature on hypnosis and ADHD. I recently began exploring the success, if any, of hypnosis in treating ADHD. The conclusion I've reached is that, while there is a wealth of information on treating inattention with hypnosis, the treatment's effectiveness is less than confident. Numerous psychologists and hypnotists employ hypnosis in their therapy of individuals with ADHD. What is not certain is whether hypnosis has any unique benefits for the inattentive symptoms observed in patients with ADHD.

Hypnosis has been used therapeutically for ages. It was first used in animal husbandry to soothe animals. It gained popularity in Europe in the 1800s and was widely and successfully used to treat post-traumatic stress syndrome during war (PTSS). Various modalities, including music, speech, magnets, paintings, and other images, have generated hypnotic states. When you enter the term "hypnotic photos" into Google, you will discover paintings and sights that have been used to induce hypnosis.

Despite a large amount of evidence demonstrating its efficacy in treating various diseases, several clinicians have dismissed hypnosis as a hoax. Many American physicians regard hypnosis as a bizarre form of theatrical performance with little practical application. Physicians in Asia have a considerably more favorable view of hypnosis. These clinicians have conducted hundreds of investigations on hypnosis, demonstrating its efficacy in treating mental health and other illnesses.

Although studies conducted in this country have demonstrated that hypnosis is successful in treating the majority of medical conditions, American and Asian medical practitioners generally agree that hypnosis is beneficial in treating depression, anxiety, and phobias. However, there is far less agreement regarding the efficacy of hypnosis in treating other disorders.

There appears to be a bias in favor of hypnosis in Asia and discrimination against hypnosis in the United States. Even well-designed random/controlled studies on hypnosis conducted in the United States, which demonstrate a reduction in symptoms in the treatment group, are questioned and scrutinized for weaknesses and limitations. The opposite appears to be true in Asian studies.

Experts in the field are keen to point out that stage hypnosis (hypnosis included in performance) is not the same as genuine hypnosis. These specialists emphasize that true hypnosis does not compel us to act against our will. While hypnotists agree that all forms of hypnosis require a mental state commonly referred to as a trance, how this trance can appear to an observer is fundamentally different from what we frequently see of hypnotized persons in films or on television.

Psychologists and hypnotists claim that individuals with ADHD are more easily hypnotized than individuals without this condition and that youngsters are more hypnotizable than adults. There are several and varied ways of hypnosis, including NLP, which employs language to produce a hypnotic state. Since its inception in the early 1970s, this method of hypnosis has grown in popularity. Self-hypnosis is another commonly available type of hypnosis in which music, images, and/or affirmations are used to establish a hypnotic state.

Instantaneous Neuronal Activation Procedure (INAP) is a type of hypnosis in which the subject is awake and alert with their eyes open. A trance condition is generated in seconds. According to proponents of this form of hypnosis, active-alert hypnosis can be as effective as trance hypnosis in curing some conditions.

When trusted hypnosis techniques are used, many studies published in reputable journals have demonstrated relief in symptoms associated with Tourette's syndrome, headaches, anxiety, aches, and depression. Studies examining how hypnosis alleviates the symptoms of various diseases revealed that hypnosis, like meditation, yoga, and exercise, can alleviate the symptoms of these conditions by restoring anomalies in the hypothalamic-pituitary-adrenal axis' ACTH-beta-endorphin functioning.

The Complete History of Hypnosis

The first kind of psychotherapy is hypnosis (Ellenberger, 1970). By examining primitive people's religious and healing practices, we can deduce the critical elements required to generate the hypnotic trance. It is conceivable to conclude that certain ceremonial behaviors existed before written history. The employment of rhythmic chanting, monotonous drumbeats, strained fixations of the eyes, and catalepsy of the rest of the body are all trance-inducing techniques in and of themselves. If we accept this concept, we can assume that hypnosis, as we now refer to it, has existed as a way of accessing the unconscious and allowing the cold to assist the conscious in achieving the desired changes and advantages for as long as we have tried to alter our behavior. Until Braid's 1842 publication, these activities would not have been referred to as hypnosis, despite their hypnotic nature.

The earliest recorded account of hypnosis cures comes from the Ebers Papyrus, which sheds light on Egyptian medicine's theories and practice before 1552 BC. The Ebers Papyrus describes a treatment in which the physician placed his hands on the patient's head and, claiming superhuman therapeutic powers, spoke unusual remedial utterances to the patient, which resulted in a cure. Both the Greeks and Romans practiced inducing sleep or relaxation states; Hippocrates highlighted the topic, stating that "despite the body's ailment, the spirit sees perfectly well with its eyes closed." Unfortunately, early Christianity saw the practice as unholy and associated it with non-Christian and prohibited religious rules, eventually leading to witchcraft.

Dr. James Braid (1775-1860), a Scottish optometrist, accidentally discovered in 1841 that a person fixating on an item may readily enter a trance state without using the mesmeric passes advocated by Dr. Mesmer. He publicized his findings, rejected Mesmer's study, and incorrectly coined the term "hypnotism" from the Greek word for "sleep."

During Braid's research into hypnosis, he formed the following ideas, most of which still stand today:
There is no great danger associated with hypnotic treatment nor pain or discomfort.

More research is necessary to understand several theoretical concepts regarding hypnosis.

Hypnosis is a powerful tool that should be limited entirely to trained professionals.

Although hypnotism could cure many diseases for which there had been no remedy, it nevertheless was no panacea. It was only a medical tool to be used in combination with other medical information and drugs to properly treat the patient.

Auguste Ambrose Liebeault (1823-1904) and Hippolyte Bernheim (1840-l919) formed the Nancy School, which was instrumental in establishing a form of hypnosis accepted in a wide variety of circles. Liebelt is frequently referred to as a simple country doctor, but by freely treating the peasants of Nancy, he amassed great experience and expertise with hypnosis. In 1860, he began his first investigation of hypnosis. In 1882, he successfully treated sciatica in a patient who had previously been unsuccessfully treated by others.

Bernheim was a sophisticated Parisian physician who began visiting Nancy regularly, and the two men became close friends and colleagues. Bernheim first published *De la Suggestion*, the first half of his book, in 1884. In 1886, the second half, *La Therapeutic Suggestion*, was published. The appearance of these two volumes rekindled interest in Liebeault's book, which had been published twenty years prior and had sold only one copy at the time.

In 1882, Jean-Martin Charcot (1835-1893) addressed the French Academy of Sciences with his results on hypnotism. Charcot believed that hypnosis was fundamentally hysteria, and many people bought into his argument because he was a neurologist. However, Charcot gained knowledge about hypnosis from his work with twelve hysterics at the Saltpetriere. Most of his subject findings were based on that small sample. The Nancy school argued against Charcot's conclusion and secured hypnosis as a natural outcome of suggestion.

Pierre Marie Félix Janet (1859-1947) was a French neurologist and psychologist who studied under Jean-Martin Charcot at

Paris's Pitié-Salpêtrière Hospital's Psychological Laboratory. He predated Sigmund Freud in some respects. Many regard Janet as the genuine founder of psychoanalysis and psychotherapy rather than Freud. He initially presented his findings in 1889 in his philosophy thesis and 1892 in his medical dissertation, *L'état Mental des Hystériques*. He was the first to link prior experiences in a subject's life and their current trauma, coining the terms *dissociation* and *subconscious*. He was responsible for hypnosis' dissociation hypothesis. This individual was first hostile to hypnosis until he found its soothing effects and ability to promote healing.

Janet began his career as a lecturer in psychology at the Sorbonne in 1898. He was named chair of experimental and comparative psychology at the Collège de France in 1902, a position he held until 1936. From 1913, he was a member of the Institut de France. He published a canonical treatise on the suggestion, *La Médecine Psychologique*, in 1923, and many definitive studies on memory between 1928 and 1932. While he authored nothing in English, his 1908 Harvard University lectures were published as *The Major Symptoms of Hysteria*, and Harvard awarded him an honorary degree in 1936.

Josef Breuer (1842-1925) was a Vienna-born Austrian physician whose writings laid the groundwork for psychoanalysis. He graduated from Vienna's Akademisches Gymnasium in 1858 and then spent a year at the university before enrolling in Vienna's medical school. He passed his medical exams in 1867 and began working at the university as an assistant to internist Johann Oppolzer. Josef Breuer discovered that while hypnotized, some persons could recollect prior occurrences, which appeared to aid in the treatment of various disorders. He referred to this as a talking cure. During World War I, the German troops used this to treat shell shock via hypnosis.

Sigmund Freud (1856-1939), the founder of psychoanalysis, experimented with hypnosis in his early work but soon became disillusioned with the concept. There is a view that he lacked the patience required for hypnosis and was an ineffective hypnotist. Between 1883 and 1887, he grew interested in and performed hypnosis, and in 1885, Freud spent time with Charcot and was quite impressed. He also translated Bernheim's *De la Suggestion* into German.

Freud and his associate, Joseph Breuer, successfully used hypnosis in psychotherapy in Vienna, and in 1895, they published their seminal, '*Studies in Hysteria*.' Freud visited Nancy in 1889 and was convinced by the 'strong mental processes that remain hidden from men's consciousness. When a female patient he had awakened from hypnosis put her arms around his neck, he discovered positive transference. "I was modest enough not to attribute the incident to my own irresistible personal desire, and I thought that I had now comprehended the nature of the enigmatic element at work behind hypnotism," Freud wrote.

Later in life, he left hypnosis, claiming it was ineffective, and devoted his efforts to developing psychoanalysis. He shifted his focus to analysis and free association; this defection was detrimental to hypnosis, particularly in the context of psychology, because it fostered permanent prejudices and misconceptions that have just recently begun to dissipate. Interest in hypnosis waned with the introduction of psychoanalysis and the use of anesthetics.

Dr. Emile Coué (1857-1926) was another early proponent of contemporary hypnosis and self-development. At the turn of the nineteenth century, he believed in auto-suggestion and the hypnotist's function as a facilitator of change and healing through the client's full participation in the hypnosis process. By 1887, Coué had developed the notion of auto-suggestion, marking the first time that ego-strengthening (a central tenet of traditional occult and shamanic techniques) was applied to modern science. He believed in the importance of the imagination in influencing a person's will and conducted tests to determine how offering suggestions to people affected their behavior. His well-known self-help slogan, "Day by day, I am improving in every aspect," is still used in the majority of self-improvement therapies.

Coué's Laws of Suggestion:
1. The Law of Concentrated Attention - "Whenever attention is concentrated on an idea over and over again, it spontaneously tends to realize itself."
2. The Law of Reverse Action - "The harder one tries to do something, the less chance one has of success."
3. The Law of Dominant Effect - "A stronger emotion tends to replace a weaker one."

Coué thought that he did not heal patients but rather aided their self-healing. He recognized the critical role of the subject's participation in hypnosis, foreshadowing the notion that there is no such thing as hypnosis, only self-hypnosis. Perhaps his most famous assertion was that the imagination is always more substantial than the will. For instance, when asked to walk over a piece of wood on the floor, most people could do so without wobbling. However, when instructed to close their eyes and envision the board suspended between two high structures, individuals always waver. Coué may also have anticipated the placebo effect, a treatment with no intrinsic value whose effectiveness is based on suggestion in which patients are told they are being given a drug that will cure them.

Dr. Oskar Vogt invented the fractionation method, and one of his students, Johannes Schultz, later introduced Autogenic Training, which many regards as a sort of self-hypnosis.

Ivan P. Pavlov (1849-1936), a Russian scientist, pioneered the study of hypnosis' concepts and methods. He is most known for discovering the Pavlovian Response, a conditioned reflex. Following World War I, hypnosis and its therapeutic applications underwent a renaissance when psychiatrists found that soldiers suffering from psychological traumas, such as paralysis and amnesia, responded effectively to hypnotism and were speedily treated.

Milton Erickson (1932-1974) was a psychologist and psychiatrist who revolutionized hypnosis by developing the art of indirect suggestion. He is widely regarded as the founder of contemporary hypnosis. Using both verbal and nonverbal pacing strategies, including metaphor, confusion, imagery, surprise, and humor, he circumvented the conscious mind. Erickson used hypnosis to assist his clients' advancement and rehabilitation throughout his career. He was an excellent and quick observer of people, capable of quickly establishing rapport with his clientele. His hypnotic techniques, today referred to as Ericksonian Hypnosis, gave modern hypnotherapy a new depth. In conjunction with Satir and Perls, his work served as the foundation for Bandler and Grinder's Neuro-Linguistic Programming (NLP).

Albert Mason was a young anesthetic working at a hospital in East Grinstead, Sussex, England, a specialty plastic surgery center following World War II. Mr. Moore, the surgeon with whom he was working, was furious one day when the skin graft he had performed on a teenage boy failed and had made problems worse. The youngster was suffering from a severe case of ichthyosis. This is typically a genetic disorder in which the patient has fewer sweat and sebaceous glands than average, resulting in dry, scaly skin. The boy's body was almost completely covered in a thick coating of hard, dry skin that frequently dripped a crimson serum. The adolescent, dubbed "the child with elephant skin," had suffered from this disease since birth and had been unable to be helped by traditional medicine. This was his second skin graft operation, but each time the new skin flared up.

Perhaps unaware of the medic's current opinion that hypnosis was not intended to be used to treat congenital disorders, Dr. Mason offered to assist the youngster. He hypnotized the youngster in front of a dozen dubious doctors. The blackened skin on his left arm crumbled and peeled away five days later, revealing reddish but otherwise normal skin beneath. After ten days, the boy's arm was completely healed.

Dr. Mason then used hypnosis on the boy's other bodily parts, obtaining extraordinary results, and the case was published in the 1952 British Medical Journal. Dr. Mason published a follow-up article three years later, finding that the results looked to be lasting. Albert was hounded by people suffering from ichthyosis from miles around, but he could never replicate the boy's achievement. Albert reasoned that he knew at that point that ichthyosis could not be treated with hypnosis and that this was either being communicated to the patient in some way or was impeding his success.

The British Parliament passed the Hypnotism Act in 1952. It was created to safeguard the public against potentially dangerous stage hypnotism activities. While hypnosis is a highly effective tool in the hands of adequately educated doctors and therapists, many believe it is far too powerful to play with for amusement purposes. Throughout history, public hypnosis demonstrations have occurred, with the presenters frequently following their performances with private consultations. However, hypnotism's image was eventually tarnished by several forgers who used simple routines and paid stooges.

The success of an American stage hypnotist, Ormond McGill, reignited interest in hypnotism. Along with pioneering hypnosis as a form of television entertainment, McGill authored what is now considered the bible of stage hypnosis, The New Encyclopedia of Stage Hypnotism and Professional Stage Hypnotism. In the United Kingdom, the return of stage hypnotism was followed by increased concern about the potential risks of stage hypnosis, prompting the introduction of the 1952 Hypnotism Act.

The Home Office established an expert panel in 1994 to look at any evidence of potential harm to those participating in public entertainments employing hypnotism and to assess the efficiency of the law governing hypnosis for entertainment. In 1995, parliament announced the publication of the expert panel's findings, which determined that "there was no evidence of considerable harm to participants in stage hypnosis, and that whatever risk that does exist is far less important than that associated in a wide variety of other activities."

Hypnosis was officially approved as a tool in medicine by the British Medical Association (BMA) in 1955.

In the USA, the Council on Medical health of the American Medical Association accepted the use of hypnotherapy in 1958.

On May 4, 1955, William J. Bryan Jr. (1924-1977), a medical doctor, a minister of religion, and an attorney, formed and became the first president of the American Institute of Hypnosis. It was created as an educational organization dedicated to advancing all stages of hypnosis in the fields of medicine and dentistry. Thus, the institute was formed to fill a void in that field. The institute included professionals from medicine, dentistry, psychology, psychiatry, and theology. It grew rapidly and eventually became the world's most prestigious educational institution devoted only to teaching hypnosis in medicine and dentistry to physicians and dentists worldwide.

In the 1970s, a breakthrough was accomplished in self-improvement and inner resource mobilization. Although it is unrelated to hypnosis, many of its approaches can be used with or as a supplement to hypnotic therapy. Information scientist, Richard Brandler, and linguistics professor, John Grindler, developed this approach. They coined the term Neuro-Linguistic Programming (NLP). It was founded in significant part on the study, comprehension, and development of Milton H. Erickson's psychotherapy methods by its two founders. NLP is a technique for personal growth that makes use of our neurology and cognitive patterns, our manner of expressing our thoughts and their influence on us, and our practices of behavior and goal setting. It has been dubbed the "ultimate brain software."

WHY LEARN HYPNOSIS? A GUIDE TO THE BENEFITS THAT HYPNOSIS CAN OFFER

I'm aware that you're intrigued about hypnosis and that you're looking for information to determine whether hypnosis can assist you in solving your problems. And I understand why I ended up in a similar predicament to yours a few years back. I was initially suspicious of hypnosis. Indeed, having witnessed several live hypnotism performances on television, I had a much better concept of hypnosis—what appeared to be a circus! This is because during a typical concert, a hypnotist requests the participation of an audience member. The hypnotist then performs hypnosis, making the is a victim of the hypnotist's so-called role of power. This implies that the hypnotized person will automatically enter hypnosis without setting resistors.

Hypnosis is used to resolve fundamental problems a person may be experiencing. And it's so long-lasting and straightforward that with just a few sessions of hypnosis, you may wave goodbye to issues like obsessive hunger, stress, hostility, and relationship difficulties.

Now, let me explain why I chose to approach and learn hypnosis. One day, at the library, I discovered a book about NLP. I randomly opened the book and had just finished a review in which the author discussed the applications of hypnosis and NLP. From that first book, the universe opened up to me and piqued my interest, and I recognized that hypnosis had the potential to improve my life. I'll offer you some examples of the difficulties I was facing at the time, and why hypnosis presented itself as a cure:

Stress: I was constantly stressed, especially about working with my clients.

- Anxiety: whenever I faced a problem of a certain magnitude, whether as a medical professional, during an interview, or when I went to a party with strangers, I was highly anxious and stressed, with a true knot in my stomach.

- Difficulty concentrating on learning a new language: for years, I put in the effort to study, but my inner voice kept telling me I was stupid, and that I was too old to learn anything new.

- Improving my connection with my partner: as a couple, we gathered both harmful and painful experiences resulting from misunderstandings that sent us away from each other over the last few years.

- Increase my determination to attain my goals: there were times in my life when I was successful, but others were unsuccessful, leaving me with little to no motivation to move forward and achieve my goals.

In my life, I've always attempted to delve deep to solve difficulties, and I've learned to trace things back to their sources. I have accomplished the same thing with hypnosis. I set out to identify the world's finest hypnotist and to learn how to use hypnosis to mesmerize others and induce an altered state of awareness in them.

I witnessed individuals who have been hypnotized and given hypnotic instructions on what should be abandoned, such as excessive stress, which is poured into a compulsive attitude toward food. These individuals were given instructions to turn to more effective coping strategies, like exercise, which made the stress disappear.

And I've seen immediate changes!

In my case, I used hypnosis to assist me in overcoming the limiting belief that I was no longer capable of learning a foreign language. As you know, less than three months after my hypnosis session, I mastered more than 80% of the language I wanted, and I'm still improving daily. And all this happened as a result of hypnosis and the benefits it had on my life and habits.

If you are still skeptical about hypnosis, let me ask you now:

"As you wait to resolve your difficulties—major or small—are you ready to turn to hypnosis to experience its benefits?"

Learning hypnosis allows you to improve yourself or the people who matter most to you and who may genuinely wish to assist you in feeling better. For instance, you may employ hypnosis in the following ways:

For your son to do better and learn to relax;
With your partner, perhaps to remove the friction torque and minor misunderstandings that are harmful to your relationship;
Or for yourself to be more serene and peaceful in your days;

To address and resolve once and for all your bad relationship with food.

Now, I believe you must learn about the benefits of hypnosis.

Chapter 6

Proof That Hypnosis Works

There are numerous divergent views regarding the validity of hypnosis as a kind of therapy. However, scientific investigations appear to have solidly established hypnosis as a legitimate treatment that is also quite successful.

It's only logical that someone would seek confirmation that an alternative treatment, such as hypnosis, actually works before attempting it. Scientific research has been conducted over the last several decades, all of which points to the same conclusion: hypnosis *does* work.

HYPNOSIS AND HEALING

In 2003, Harvard Medical School conducted an experiment to determine the effect of hypnosis on the speed of bone regeneration. The study treated twelve persons with fractured ankles, half of whom received conventional treatment and half of whom received hypnosis in addition to traditional therapy.

The results were astounding, with those who experienced hypnosis healing in six weeks compared to those who did not, who needed eight and a half weeks to heal. The proof that hypnosis works in this instance is self-evident. Simply by including hypnosis into their therapy, persons with shattered bones healed almost 25% faster than those who only received conventional care.

This study may be of particular interest to athletes who want to expedite the recuperation process to return to training and competition.

HYPNOSIS AND PAIN CONTROL

Researchers at the University of Iowa Health Science Relations used functional magnetic resonance imaging (fMRI) scans to determine the impact of hypnosis on pain control. The study discovered that hypnotized participants felt minor discomfort when exposed to heat than those who did not receive hypnosis. Brain scans confirmed this finding, which revealed considerably different patterns of brain activity in hypnotized volunteers compared to those who were not. This strongly suggests that hypnosis suppresses pain signals from the brain.

HYPNOSIS SHOWS ON BRAIN SCANS

In 2009, researchers at Hull University discovered that hypnosis had a noticeable influence when brain activity was scanned. As some skeptics assert, this demonstrates that hypnosis is not a placebo effect.

Dr. Michael Heap, the study's psychologist, determined that hypnosis prepares the mind for suggestion. This study established that hypnosis works and thoroughly explained how it works. After priming the mind for suggestion, a hypnotist can assist their client in achieving their goals.

I have mentioned only three of the numerous research conducted on hypnosis, but there have been many more. There is evidence that hypnosis is effective for weight loss, IBS treatment, skin disorders, and enhanced fertility.

Perhaps the most conclusive proof that hypnosis works is to give it a try for yourself. Additionally, anecdotal data supports the effectiveness of hypnosis. Even celebrities like Matt Damon and Ellen DeGeneres have admitted that hypnosis assisted them in quitting smoking.

DOES HYPNOSIS WORK FOR WEIGHT LOSS?

Hypnosis inspires pictures of a bearded man with piercing dark eyes and a captivating deep voice swinging a pendulum back and forth, saying, "You are becoming sleepy." Hypnosis is widely misunderstood, and for most individuals, their only exposure to it will be through a Las Vegas stage act. However, two wholly different beasts are stage hypnosis for entertainment purposes and hypnotherapy for behavior modification. Could genuine hypnosis assist you in losing weight?

I've wondered about the same issue for decades since I began bodybuilding.

Dr. Judd Biasiotto published multiple books about the mind in sports in the late 1980s, including one titled *Hypnotize Me and Make Me Great.*

That 70-page book, which has since been discontinued (but still has a special place on my shelf), was one of the publications that piqued my interest in mind power and hypnosis.

For anyone unfamiliar with strength sports, Dr. Judd is the man who squatted 605 pounds at a body weight of 132 pounds—an incredible feat, as any powerlifter will attest. When a world-class lifter with a Ph.D. in sports psychology asserts that hypnosis has merit and that his mental training routine was vital in his success, a desperate teenage wannabe bodybuilder is intrigued!

After all these years, my fascination with hypnosis and the mind's powers has never dimmed. I've used self-hypnosis and hypnosis CDs to improve gym performance, generate maximum intensity during workouts, and push through the pain barrier. While I do not believe hypnosis is magical, it has been beneficial. Additionally, I think that a comprehensive mental training program, which may involve hypnotherapy, can make or break the effectiveness of a weight-loss program and provide sportspeople with a competitive edge.

Any seasoned coach will tell you that it makes no difference which diet or workout program you follow if you cannot adhere to it regularly. Numerous issues, such as non-compliance, self-sabotage, inconsistency, and lack of drive, are psychological, not physical.

One common myth regarding hypnosis is that you would lose control of your faculties or that it is some form of "mind control." This is not true any more than it is true that your family, friends, classmates, or culture control your thinking.

The fact is that the mind is susceptible to suggestion (particularly the mind of a very young child), and everything is hypnosis in that sense. In some ways, reading the newspaper or watching television is hypnosis or mental programming. Unless you consciously choose to be unique and become what you want to be, you are programmed to conform to cultural conventions.

Another source of hypnosis misunderstanding stems from stage hypnosis, which has little to do with personal change hypnotherapy. The stage hypnotist selects the most susceptible members of his audience—who also happen to be willing participants—and then causes some hypnotic event for entertainment purposes.

As it is employed in personal transformation work, hypnosis is a calm state of altered consciousness and heightened focus in which the conscious mind withdraws, allowing the hypnotherapist's message to more easily reach your subconscious. When the subconscious receives the news, it stimulates positive behaviors, which is why hypnosis is merely a tool for behavior modification.

Self-hypnosis is as simple as taking long, deep breaths, relaxing (sometimes using progressive muscle relaxation techniques), and then performing your visualization or repeating affirmations, or even listening to your own self-created affirmations tape.

While some individuals report significant success using hypnosis, others do not. The mixed results are due to the practitioner, while others are due to the topic. What results may you anticipate from hypnosis? Could hypnosis assist you in losing weight or altering other aspects of your body?

I believe in a mind-body connection and feel that it is feasible for the brain, central nervous system, and subconscious mind to physically speak to the various cells in your body, which may play a role in healing. I believe that the human body is an extraordinary self-healing machine equipped with its own natural medicine.

I believe it isn't easy to prove. Still, given the existence of a real discipline dedicated to this issue (psychoneuroimmunology), the scientific community appears to believe in the mind-body connection enough to commit time, money, and resources to investigating it. There are many intriguing and realistic hypotheses. Additionally, we must examine the placebo effect, demonstrating how a thought may alter biology in absolutely remarkable ways.

That said, I believe you should approach hypnosis with care and interest. To begin, and maybe entirely, you should view hypnosis as a tool for behavior modification. When considering a hypnosis claim, you should consider whether the claim may be reached through a change in your conduct.

For instance, if someone advertises hypnosis as a means of increasing muscle mass, is it feasible that your behavior may change in such a way that you build more muscle? Yes, it is. Hypnosis may assist you in altering your eating habits, or you may simply push yourself harder in the gym. Thus, muscle gain occurs due to behavioral modification—eating better and training harder—rather than as a function of hypnosis.

It's the same with weight loss: Will hypnosis miraculously boost your metabolism as a result of a mind-body connection? While I prefer to keep an open mind, I highly doubt it and am skeptical of hypnotherapists who claim to be able to hypnotize you and increase your metabolism. If it is possible, I doubt it will ever be proved scientifically. Thus, it may eventually come down to your willingness to believe the claims.

WHAT ABOUT WEIGHT LOSS?

Although the results are inconclusive, some clinical psychology research published in peer-reviewed journals demonstrates healthy weight loss using hypnosis. In part 2 of this series, we'll learn more about the findings of those investigations.

Even more enlightening, in my opinion, are certain documented occurrences of medical hypnosis, which vary from simple pain alleviation during dental work to surgery performed without anesthetic (which is pretty freaky if you think about it). The mind does affect the physical body.

Hypnosis sessions or hypnosis CDs can be a beneficial supplement to comprehensive fitness, nutrition, and lifestyle program for some people, if a credible and qualified hypnotherapist conducts them.

Even better, I believe the ideal session would incorporate conscious coaching and teaching in addition to classic hypnosis, rather than simply being a passive scenario in which you listen and expect your mind to be positively trained.

However, I believe this is why weight reduction hypnosis CDs sell like hotcakes, as they are frequently promoted under the guise of doing nothing. Simply listen and lose weight—the ideal fast fix. I don't believe it's that straightforward. If you genuinely want to succeed, you must assume responsibility for change, take an active role in its creation, and lean toward action. You must work on both the physical and mental levels concurrently, rather than simply thinking positively or relying on self-help CDs of any kind.

While I believe hypnosis is a great tool, most of the time, at the end of the day, programming your mind for success comes down to what you say to yourself (and see/read/ hear). While you cannot work with a hypnotherapist every day of your life, you speak to yourself constantly throughout the day, and repetition is a proven method of conditioning the mind.

When you think about it, the way you speak to yourself most of the time *is* self-hypnosis.

If you already have an organized training and eating plan in place but are having difficulty changing your behavior, hypnotherapy or positive mental programming CD's may be worth adding to your mental training toolkit.

YOUR QUESTIONS ABOUT HYPNOSIS ANSWERED

There is so much misinformation about hypnosis circulating on the Internet that I felt compelled to correct the record. After all, knowledge is a beautiful thing. Thus, the following are straightforward responses to the most often asked questions about hypnosis:

Does Hypnosis Work?

Definitely! Hypnosis's modern applications have elevated it to a respected and esteemed member of the healing arts. Historically held beliefs and misconceptions about hypnosis have been superseded by its ethical application in law, medicine, psychology, dentistry, education, sports, and self-improvement and growth. Its use has helped millions. Hundreds of thousands, if not millions, of Americans, use hypnosis every day.

Hypnosis has been clinically validated and evaluated. In 1958, the American Medical Association approved hypnosis. Harvard University, Seton Hall School of Medicine, Stanford University, Columbia College of Physicians and Surgeons, and most other major universities in the United States now teach hypnosis.

What is the Subconscious Mind?

Our subconscious controls our behavior, memory, creativity, and emotion. Additionally, it has an effect on every system in the body. It is suggestive. The subconscious mind does not reason; it simply follows instructions, whether good or bad. No matter how much work and determination you devote to changing behavior, the subconscious will undermine you if there's a conflict. It simply does not comprehend. It is in desperate need of reeducation! That is the purpose of hypnosis.

Can Children Be Hypnotized?

Definitely! All ages of children make fantastic subjects. Numerous difficulties youngsters develop can be avoided via the expert application of hypnosis. Additionally, it provides them with a significant advantage, whether it comes to education or athletic training. Memory, discipline, confidence, motivation, and self-control, to name a few, can all be strengthened quickly.

Chapter 7

Hypnosis And The Mind

The human mind can be classified into three distinct components: the unconscious, the subconscious, and the conscious.

In comparison to a computer, they are: **Unconscious = operating system Subconscious = hard drive Conscious = RAM**

Each component performs various functions.
The unconscious mind controls your body's autonomic systems, such as the circulatory system, in the same way that a computer's operating system controls its fundamental functions.

The subconscious mind functions similarly to a hard drive, holding files of all types, from a complete memory bank of your past to your emotional spectrum, to its most critical function: safeguarding you at all costs.

The conscious mind is our simple mind; it makes instant decisions about what to wear, eat, and drink daily. The gatekeeper determines which data is to be acted upon on a moment-by- moment basis. It is the mind with which you are currently reading this book, and it is tasked with comparing, reasoning, and explaining. Together with the critical factor, these talents are bypassed during hypnosis.

The subconscious mind's importance

To make changes to a file on your computer, you must first open the original file. The subconscious is where original files are stored in the human mind. To obtain access, we must bypass the conscious mind and directly contact the subconscious. In other words, one strategy for achieving positive changes in the present is to mitigate the previous negative. We do not alter the memories; instead, we enhance your perception of them.

This upgrading can occur only in the subconscious, as that is where memories are stored, and it can happen only by bypassing the conscious mind, which can be accomplished only under hypnosis.

Why? That is what is effective. Hypnosis is unique in that it briefly disengages the conscious mind.

Your Mind Must Defend You; Both Good and Bad News

At all times, all levels of your mind attempt to safeguard you as best they can. And this is particularly true of the subconscious.

It must safeguard you at all costs, and to do so; it may even deceive you, or more precisely, your conscious mind. It may make false statements about you or others, and it may even make false statements to your hypnotist while you are in a trance. It may obliterate memories. This is because once it accepts undesirable habits in the name of your safety, it becomes attached to them. Several examples include the following:

Smoking
Being obese
Declining success
Biting your fingernails
Spending compulsively

You may reasonably inquire how compulsive spending can safeguard you. It diverts your attention. Misdirection is one extremely efficient method by which your subconscious shields you by controlling overpowering emotions.

You may reasonably inquire how declining to be successful might protect you. It constrains you. Another method to protect yourself is to limit your risk exposure.

When such preventive measures fail to meet your current needs, you desire to change.

Hypnosis suspends the conscious mind, modifies the subconscious mind, and results in a change.

How Hypnosis Improves the Quality of Your Files

Hypnosis can alter how you perceive your memories and, therefore, yourself. We do not change the events themselves; instead, we transform your perception of them and modify your daily existence.

By gaining access to the original information kept in the subconscious, you can see all the reasons why your mind defines your habits for your safety. Together, we may upgrade those behaviors when the need for that protection has passed. You are no longer amid the event that caused you such distress.

Your conscious mind does not have full access to your memory files; this is not its function. This is why merely discussing change is useless in enacting it. Speaking occurs within the conscious mind. Change occurs within our subconscious mind.

And herein lies the rub: the subconscious mind has the upper hand over the conscious mind. It is far more significant, stronger, and powerful than the previous one. This is why dieters struggle so severely with willpower. Unless the subconscious mind agrees to a balanced diet and a stabilized body weight, your best intentions will be short-lived due to the subconscious mind's override.

Emotions are a function of the subconscious and are kept there. When you have an emotional response to danger, whether actual or imagined, those feelings are felt and stored in your subconscious. Hypnosis allows you to access those suppressed emotions, enhances your experience of them, and leads to altered behavior.

You must first provide yourself permission to change. You must be motivated to change. You must desire hypnosis. And this includes overcoming one's fear of hypnosis.

HOW TO USE SELF HYPNOSIS TO
ACHIEVE YOUR GOALS

Self-hypnosis can be used to alter a variety of aspects of your life. Self-hypnosis can be used to alleviate negative emotions connected with unpleasant memories. You can use self-hypnosis to eliminate negative thoughts and replace them with positive ones. Therefore, if self-hypnosis is so effective, why do some people not benefit from it?

The simple reason is that they are not adequately using self-hypnosis!

To get the most out of any self-hypnosis session, you must first understand why you are using it. Before attempting self-hypnosis, you must have an objective; otherwise, all you will achieve is deep relaxation. Establish a self-hypnosis objective!

This self-hypnosis objective should be concise and specific. By committing your declaration of intent to writing, you solidify your mental image of what you want and give your subconscious mind something to work toward. You establish a self-hypnosis objective!

Ensure that any self-hypnosis program you create does not contain anything you do not desire. Make your self-hypnosis goal positive and affirming of success. For instance, stating "I am no longer overweight" or "I have no outstanding bills" is not an appropriate way to phrase your self-hypnosis objective. When you concentrate on not being overweight, your mind conjures up an image of being obese. When considering having no unpaid bills, it is necessary to consider unpaid bills. This is true of everything in life, but it is critical in self-hypnosis!

The mind is image-based! To illustrate this argument, consider your kitchen. What happened to the cooker? Are you in possession of a refrigerator? What shade is it? Is the door left- or right-handed?

Can you see that a visual recall of your house is required to answer these questions?

As a result, you must construct a written statement that focuses entirely on the things you desire and makes no mention of the things you no longer wish to experience. Positive comments such as "I easily achieve my optimum weight" rather than "I am no longer overweight" are examples.

You may ensure that the only image that forms in your mind is a pleasant one by following this advice. When you recollect these images during self-hypnosis, you are teaching your subconscious mind to assist you in creating them.

Now that you've created a written statement outlining your goals for self-hypnosis sessions, you can become more detailed. By developing a clear vision of what you want, you can use it to reprogram your mind during a self-hypnosis session.

Now read the statement you created and become aware of the mental images appearing. Increase their size, brightness, and emotional impact. Adjust the mental scene until it is precise. Continue to alter it until it makes you feel remarkable.

The written phrase and mental image, combined with the positive feelings, form your success blueprint, which you will implant into your mind during self-hypnosis.

There are many excellent self-hypnosis recordings available for specific purposes (as well as a plethora of poor ones), and if you have a goal in mind, it should be pretty straightforward to find one that fits. If, however, you choose to experiment with self-hypnosis without using a recording, you may use the self-hypnosis script below. Simply continue practicing self-hypnosis daily until you achieve your goal.

Self-Hypnosis Script:
Before beginning your self-hypnosis session, take a comfortable position, sitting or lying down. Assure yourself that you will not be disturbed.

To begin the self-hypnosis session, focus your attention on a point on the wall or ceiling just above eye level. Maintain a straight head so that you do not have to lift your eyes.

For several seconds, strain your toes and then release the tension, allowing them to relax. This enables you to distinguish between tension and relaxation. Following that, pressure and rest your lower legs, followed by your upper legs. Repeat this procedure for each muscle group in your body until your face and scalp are completely soothed.

After a few moments, your eyes will begin to feel tired from the strain, and you can close them. This is a technique used during self-hypnosis induction. While taking deep breaths, mentally count down from ten to one. Then, visualize a steep staircase ahead of you and walk down it into the darkness. Count backward from five to one.

Now, see a ten-step twisting staircase in front of you. Take a deep breath as you descend the stairway. You are in a trance and your self-hypnosis has begun by this point.

You will program your subconscious mind while in this stage of self-hypnosis. Recall the mental image you formed before. View it in all its glory. Now, play the scene and imagine yourself engaging with the characters. Once you begin to experience positive emotions, enter the film. Enter the envisioned you and assume their role. How does it feel to be a living embodiment of that image?

Permit yourself to remain immersed in the mental film for as long as it seems comfortable. Simply count up from one to ten when you are ready to exit self-hypnosis. Begin to become aware of your surroundings and any sounds that may be audible. Then, you should open your eyes. Your self-hypnosis session is now complete.

CAN YOU FIND LOVE THROUGH HYPNOTHERAPY?

While obtaining affection is one of life's greatest pleasures, it is frequently easier said than done. Finding this is challenging; remaining in love is perhaps even more so. Unsurprisingly, Rachel Crethar's job as an RTT (Rapid Transformation Therapy) hypnotherapist frequently involves working with romantic relationship concerns. "Forging a meaningful connection is inextricably linked to our struggles with self-esteem. 'How can you expect someone else to love you if you can't love yourself is a cliché for a reason," she argues. However, improving one's self-esteem is not as simple as posting affirmations on the refrigerator. Here, she discusses why RTT is an effective technique for developing a healthy romantic connection and what prompted her to create Higher Ground: Love.

FIRST, FOR THE UNBEGINNER, WHAT EXACTLY IS RTT, AND HOW DOES IT WORK?

"Through hypnotherapy, RTT assists you in revisiting the tales, language, and experiences that are impeding your progress or in which you've developed beliefs that are no longer benefiting you," Rachel adds. "From this vantage point, RTT enables you to update your calendar in real-time, allowing you to rewrite history in your own life."

WHAT ARE THE MOST COMMON BELIEFS YOU SEE CAN STOP CUSTOMERS FROM CALLING FOR A HEALTHY RELATIONSHIP?

"Feeling unlovable, believing that love is hard to obtain, or believing that love isn't available for someone like me are all problems that arise," Rachel continues. "Plus, issues such as 'no nice men left' and trust issues can be significant roadblocks."

WHY IS RTT SO EFFECTIVE IN HELPING THE CALL IN A ROMANTIC RELATIONSHIP?

"We are in the theta brain wave state between the ages of 0 and 7 (the same state we access through meditation or hypnosis). And throughout those formative years, we're like sponges, soaking up everything—whether it's directly related to us or simply observing how grownups interact with one another.

"The problem with this - and the reason why revisiting our opinions is critical - is that we are creating beliefs with a child's mind and lack perspective." of understanding, for example, that our mother suffered from postpartum depression and so paid little care to us during our first year, or that our father's departure had nothing to do with us, but rather with his inability to overcome his problems.

"Even as adults, it's tremendously restorative to realize how these stories are hurting you now and rewrite them to reflect what's true for you now, not when you were three or four."

Chapter 8

Some Life Story about Hypnosis Love

About Kristin Rivas:

Kristin Rivas is a Seattle-based Certified Hypnotist. She is the host of Mind Talk on KKNW 1150 AM's Chat With Women Network. Her interest in hypnosis stems from a profoundly personal and transformative changing experience.

Before hypnosis, Kristin's life had been ravaged by disease, with up to nine pseudo seizures each day. She was forced to walk in a wheelchair or with the assistance of a cane while wearing a helmet. The Mayo Clinic diagnosed Kristin with P.T.S.D., Conversion Disorder, and Major Depressive Disorder following neurological testing. Medications and other forms of therapy failed until a single hypnosis session resulted in the complete disappearance of all unpleasant symptoms. After being treated by Dr. Jon Connelly, Kristin became a Certified Hypnotist, the originator of Rapid Trauma Resolution Therapy. Additionally, she has had training from Jon Overdurf, Igor

Ledochowski, and Don Mottin. In 2009, she joined the National Guild of Hypnotists, the International Medical, Dental, and Hypnotherapy Association, and the International Association of Counselors and Therapists.

Kristin relocated to Seattle in 2010 from Orlando, Florida, where she has established a new life, which includes a hypnosis business. Kristin supports hypnosis as a viable form of assistance and healing for individuals in need. Kristin aspires to continue pursuing her heart's desire of assisting people in overcoming obstacles that have impeded them. Whether it's stress or pain management, recovering from heartbreak, a loved one's death, or other traumatic experiences, breaking bad habits, reducing weight, sleeping comfortably, or overcoming fears, Mind Talk Hypnosis is a tool for individuals in need of healing.

Milton H Erickson's Self-Hypnosis And Trance Experience: Milton H. Erickson taught us some truths about how hypnotherapy is ineffective without trance induction. He claimed that regardless of how receptive a client is to enter a deep trance, the session is worthless and considered meaningless if the hypnotherapist lacks the appropriate instruments to initiate one. To produce magic, a hypnotherapist must first recognize the symptoms of being in a trance-like condition.

Milton H. Erickson proposed several markers that a person is in a trance. Additionally, he proposed stages in which individuals progress from trance induction to a deep hypnotic state. Age regression is a critical sign of hypnosis. Much hypnotherapy involves the individual returning to a specific stage or age in the past. Subjects modify their behavior and respond appropriately by acting similarly to how they performed throughout that stage of their lives.

According to Milton H. Erickson, a regression cannot be acted out or feigned. This is especially true when a hypnotherapist has established a patient's behavior based on their history. And it will be uncomfortable and embarrassing to behave foolishly or childishly if a patient behaves out as if he has regressed when he has not. This indicates that regression can stem from the unconscious. Critical behaviors such as worry, uneasiness, humiliation, and embarrassment can never be played out, as they are identified and acted out only in the unconscious mind. Another indicator is anesthesia, a lack of feeling caused by a transition from awareness to introspective functioning. This is due to the state of relaxation induced by trance during hypnosis. The individual will now place a greater emphasis on the unconscious than on external cues. Anesthesia does not imply disorientation in terms of time and place. It only directs the patient's attention to the hypnotist's instructions and the corresponding changes he will make through his unconscious.

According to Milton H. Erickson, the final indicator is catalepsy, a state in which a person's sensations are suspended, muscle rigidity is present, and a fixed posture is displayed. This occurs when a person is in a trance-like state and is more receptive to modifying behavioral reactions. Catalepsy is a condition that can be induced via suggestion. Hypnotists can suggest that a patient put down a levitating hand or close or open their eyes.

A series of questions should be asked for a hypnotist to go from relaxation to profound trance. These questions are tailored to the patient's current status. Subsequent suggestions should be made regarding the individual's willingness to accept or reject the hypnotherapist's influence. It is important to remember that practitioners should work with the resistance, not against it, to avoid interfering with the process of deepening the trance.

Milton H. Erickson asserts that the key to rapid hypnotic inductions is to work with the patients, not the other way around. While flexibility with recommendations is necessary for speedy change, it is also critical to remember that working at the patient's pace yields the most promising results.

Conclusion

Whether you are dating, starting something fresh, or have been with a partner for years, there is always the potential for improvement and development; the human heart has an infinite capacity for love. It is a reality of human nature that we attract what we project. Wherever you walk, develop the habit of projecting an unconditional good emotion of love to everyone you pass. Compliments are well received, and your kindness will frequently be returned to you. Similarly, be kind to yourself by learning to accept praises. Relationship issues are often the result of divergent perspectives, either because others fail to live up to our expectations or because we fail to live up to theirs. Consider the white light streaming from your heart engulfing others and cultivate an intense love for them. Compassionately empathize with their hardships and difficulties, viewing their flaws and deficiencies as symptoms of their life's problems. While in this deeply relaxed state, connect with a strong sense of love and compassion for others. Additionally, you might construct some affirmations at this stage to reinforce your feelings of love and compassion.

If you enjoyed this title and would like to read about other topics that have changed my life, please check out my new books on Amazon or my website: www.my-mindguide.com.

Also, let's stay connected on social media. Please drop a line on Facebook or Instagram and stay tuned for updates! You're welcome to share your thoughts with me directly as well: gassner@my-mindguide.com. In return, I'll send you a gorgeous infographic that you can cut out and frame.

Also, please leave a review on Amazon, as this will help me reach an even broader audience. Thank you so much for your time, insight, and undying hunger for knowledge!

I want to say thank you to all my colleagues, clients, friends, and family members, who have all contributed to what I am now.

I also want to say thank you to Gabriel Palacios, the king of hypnotherapy and a Swiss bestseller author who taught this old fox new tricks, letting me deep-dive into the mystery of hypnotherapy. I learned so much along the journey that I'm now a certified master-hypnosis coach and conversation coach myself!

Furthermore, I want to say thank you to the fantastic teachers of SAMYANA/Bali who trained me to become a certified yoga and meditation teacher.

Last but not least, I want to give a special thanks to my master-teacher Eckhard Wunderle, who's close to a saint to me. He introduced me to the world of meditation and let me discover all the wonders it has to offer. I couldn't be prouder about having received my certification as a meditation teacher from directly from him at the Institut für Spirituelle Psychologie.

Peace, love, and happiness to all of you—until next time!

AUTHOR BIO

Kurt Friedrich Gassner is an Austrian self-improvement author who empowers his readers to better navigate the intricacies of the unconscious mind. Through his lived experience and extensive knowledge of cutting-edge psychology, he helps people actualize their fullest potential. What started as writing for his peers in exchange for drawings at the age of 14 and later working as a professional copywriter, ultimately turned into becoming the Creative Director of multiple international agencies and the author of multiple self-help books.

However, writing isn't this entrepreneurial spirit's sole passion; Kurt has also been a serial founder (My Mind Guide and Trendguide Capital, to name a few) and Business Angel, garnering four decades' worth of expertise in the global advertising and brand consulting sectors. As a result, he has earned numerous awards in the areas of creative directing, direct marketing, and training and became a self-made millionaire. Utilizing his free time during the global lockdown, he even immersed himself in hypnotherapy and is now a Licensed Hypnotherapist, Yoga Instructor, and Meditation Teacher.

When he isn't running his businesses, consulting with leaders, or writing about the unconscious mind, you can find this globetrotter traveling around the world, golfing, biking in the Alps, attending the opera, or hiking. He is also the proud father of two successful children and happily married to his wonderful spouse of 37 years. Currently, he splits his time between Munich, Germany, and Kirchberg, Austria.

Throughout his life of innumerable toughs and crests, Kurt Friedrich Gassner has continued to live by the following motto unyieldingly: "Never stop! The best is yet to come…" And it is through his unwavering determination and perseverance that he has led a life of personal prosperity, learning countless invaluable lessons along the way. To him, a life lived without sharing one's acquired wisdom isn't a fulfilling one, so he creates books as a way of giving back and making this world a better place than when he first entered it. Some of his publications include The Power of Forgiveness, Lie or Die, Soul-Match, Can You Inherit a Poisoned Mind? And The Power of Poverty. When he was 30, he wrote a best-selling children's book that sold over one million copies and was used in kindergartens in German-speaking countries. Over a dozen other psychology-related books are presently in the works. Visit Kurt's official website to unleash your inner power and harness it for your greater good: gassner@my-mindguide.com

SELF-EMPOWERMENT BOOKS

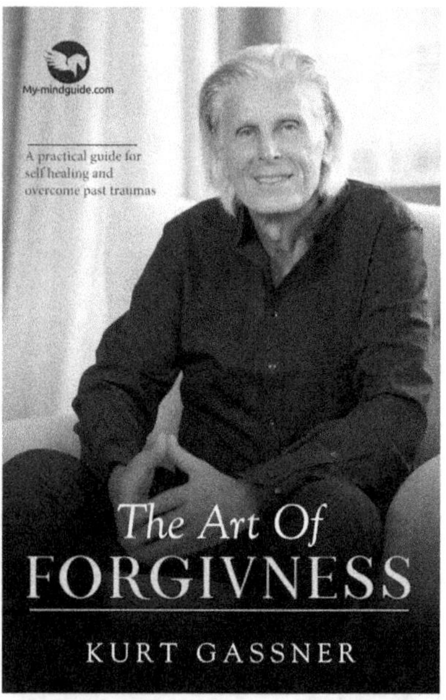

SELF-EMPOWERMENT BOOKS

SELF-EMPOWERMENT BOOKS

SELF-EMPOWERMENT BOOKS

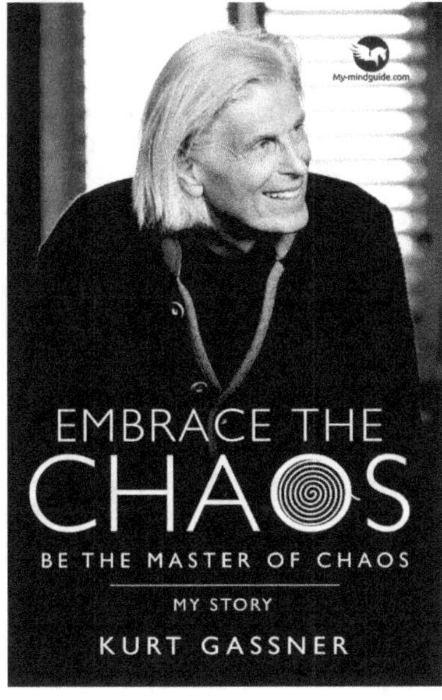

SELF-EMPOWERMENT BOOKS

SELF-EMPOWERMENT BOOKS

SELF-EMPOWERMENT BOOKS

CHILDREN BOOKS

SELF-EMPOWERMENT BOOKS

SELF-EMPOWERMENT BOOKS

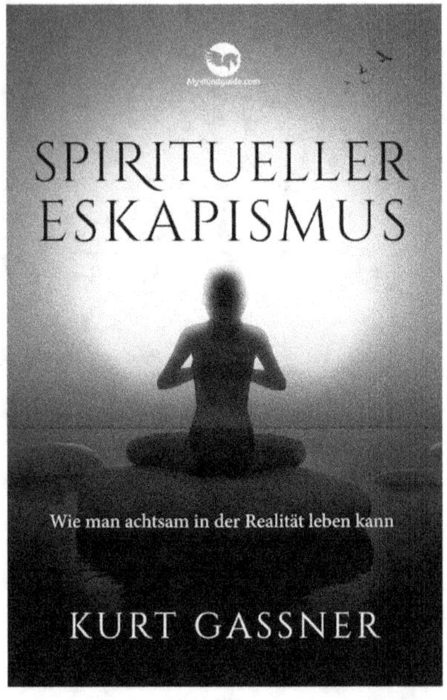

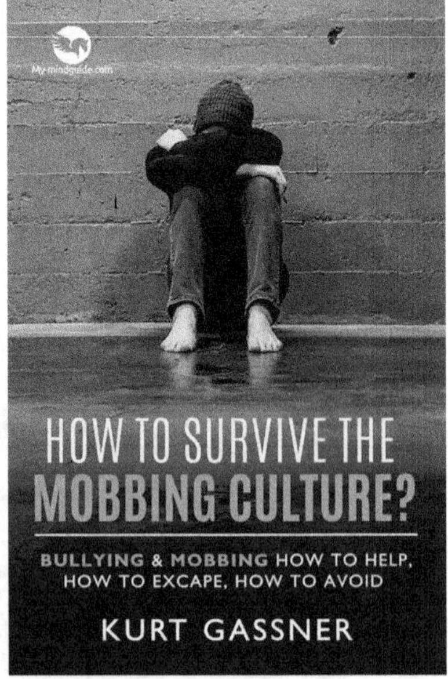

SELF-EMPOWERMENT BOOKS

MINDFUL BUSINESS BOOKS

MINDFUL BUSINESS BOOKS

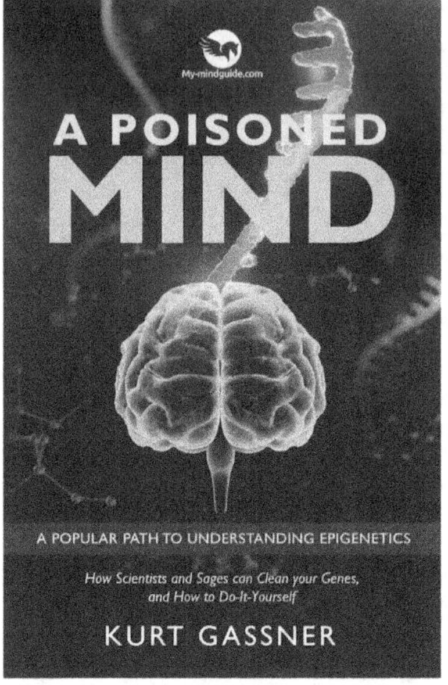

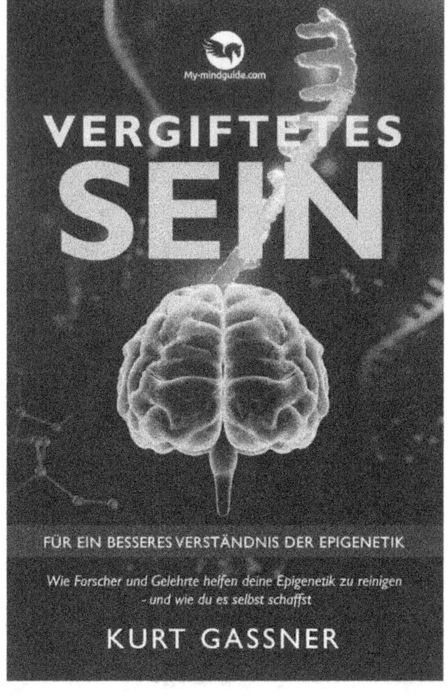

My-mindguide.com
REINVENT
YOURSELF TODAY
A GUIDE TO CLAIMING NEWFOUND JOY
BY FOLLOWING YOUR PASSIONS
KURT GASSNER

My-mindguide.com
ERFINDE
DICH NEU - NOCH HEUTE!
DER LEITFADEN ZUR LEBENSFREUDE DURCH
DEN FOKUS AUF DEINE LEIDENSCHAFTEN
KURT GASSNER

My-mindguide.com
START-UP 70
THE GUIDE TO GETTING STARTED
IN YOUR 60S, 70S, AND BEYOND
KURT GASSNER

My-mindguide.com
NEUSTART MIT 70
DEIN LEITFADEN FÜR EINEN ERFOLGREICHEN
LEBENSABSCHNITT JENSEITS DER 70
KURT GASSNER

MINDFUL BUSINESS BOOKS

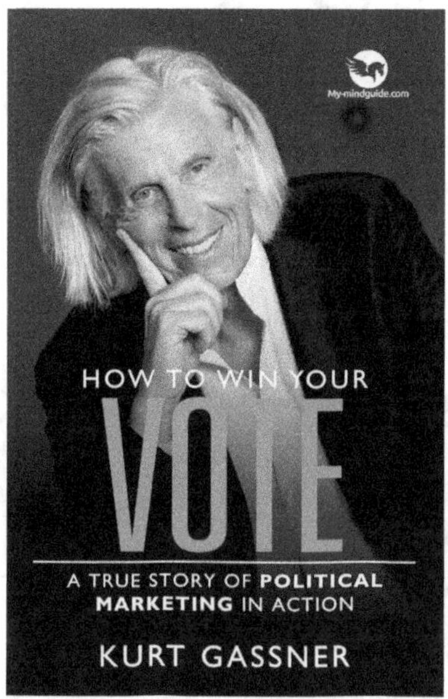

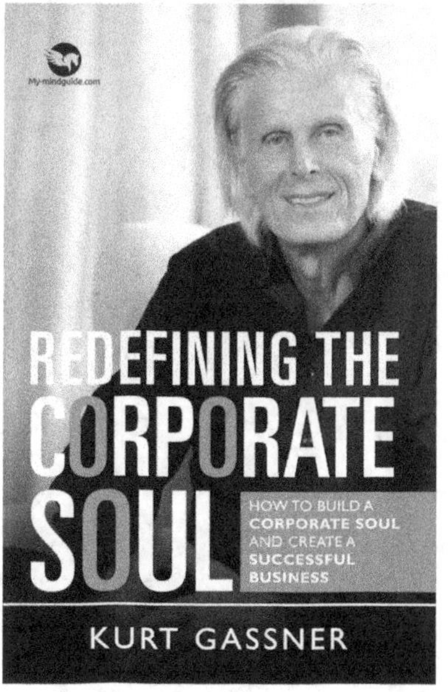

BESTSELLING AUTHOR OF
The Art Of
FORGIVNESS
AMAZON
#1
BESTSELLER
My-mindguide.com
A practical guide for
self healing and
overcome past traumas
The Art Of
FORGIVNESS
KURT GASSNER
The Art Of
FORGIVNESS
KURT GASSNER

You Can reach Author's Wikipedia